Francois Fenelon

Pathways To The Past

Each volume stands alone as an Individual Book
Each volume stands together with others
to enhance the value of your collection

Build your Personal, Pastoral or Church Library
Pathways To The Past contains an ever-expanding list of
Christendom's most influential authors

Augustine of Hippo
Athanasius
E. M. Bounds
John Bunyan
Robert Lewis Darby
Brother Lawrence
Jessie Penn-Lewis
Bernard of Clairvaux
Andrew Murray
Watchman Nee
Arthur W. Pink
Thomas Watson
Hannah Whitall Smith
R. A. Torrey
A. W. Tozer
Jean-Pierre de Caussade
And many, many more.

THE EXISTENC OF GOD
FRANCOIS FENELON

Francois Fenelon

The Existence Of God
Francois Fenelon

Published By Parables
February, 2029

All Rights Reserved. No part of this book may be reproduced or utilized in any form or by any means, electronic or mechanical, including photocopying, recording, or by any information storage and retrieval system, without permission in writing from the author.

    ISBN 978-1-951497-34-7
    Printed in the United States of America

Readers should be aware that Internet Web sites offered as citations and/or sources for further information may have been changed or disappeared between the time this was written and the time it is read.

The Existenc Of God
Francois Fenelon

Francois Fenelon

INTRODUCTION

An ancestor of the French divine who under the name of Fénelon has made for himself a household name in England as in France, was Bertrand de Salignac, Marquis de la Mothe Fénelon, who in 1572, as ambassador for France, was charged to soften as much as he could the resentment of our Queen Elizabeth when news came of the massacre of St. Bartholomew. Our Fénelon, claimed in brotherhood by Christians of every denomination, was born nearly eighty years after that time, at the château of Fénelon in Perigord, on the 6th of August, 1651. To the world he is Fénelon; he was François de Salignac de la Mothe Fénelon to the France of his own time.

Fénelon was taught at home until the age of twelve, then sent to the University of Cahors, where he began studies that were continued at Paris in the Collège du Plessis. There he fastened upon theology, and there he preached, at the age of fifteen, his first sermon. He entered next into the seminary of Saint Sulpice, where he took holy orders in the year 1675, at the age of twenty-four. As a priest, while true to his own Church, he fastened on Faith, Hope, and Charity as the abiding forces of religion, and for him also the greatest of these was Charity.

During the next three years of his life Fénelon was among the young priests who preached and catechised in the church of St. Sulpice and laboured in the parish. He wrote for St. Sulpice Litanies of the Infant Jesus, and had thought of going out as missionary to the Levant. The Archbishop of Paris, however, placed him at the head of a community of "New Catholics," whose function was to confirm new converts in their faith, and help to bring into the fold those who appeared willing to enter. Fénelon took part also in some of the Conferences on Scripture that were held at Saint Germain and Versailles between 1672 and 1685. In 1681 an uncle, who was Bishop of Sarlat, resigned in Fénelon's favour the Deanery of Carenas, which produced an annual income of three or four thousand livres. It was while he held this office that Fénelon published a book on the "Education of Girls," at the request of the Duchess of Beauvilliers, who asked for guidance in the education of her children.

Fénelon sought the friendship of Bossuet, who revised for him his next book, a "Refutation of the System of Malebranche concerning Nature and Grace." His next book, written just before the Revocation of the Edict of Nantes in 1685, opposed the lawfulness of the ministrations of the Protestant clergy; and after the Edict, Fénelon was, on the recommendation of Bossuet, placed at the head of the Catholic mission to Poitou. He brought to his work of conversion or re-conversion Charity, and a spirit of concession that brought on him the attacks of men unlike in temper.

When Louis XIV. placed his grandson, the young Duke of Burgundy, under the care of the Duke of Beauvilliers, the Duke of Beauvilliers chose Fénelon for teacher of the pupil who was heir presumptive to the throne. Fénelon's "Fables" were written as part of his educational work. He wrote also for the young Duke of Burgundy his "Télémaque"—used only in MS.—and his "Dialogues of the Dead." While thus living in high favour at Court, Fénelon sought nothing for himself or his friends, although at times he was even in want of money. In 1693—as preceptor of a royal prince rather than as author—Fénelon was received into the French Academy. In 1694 Fénelon was made Abbot of Saint-Valery, and at the end of that year he wrote an anonymous letter to Louis XIV. upon wrongful wars and other faults committed in his reign. A copy of it has been found in Fénelon's handwriting. The king may not have read it, or may not have identified the author, who was not stayed by it from promotion in February of the next year (1695) to the Archbishopric of Cambray. He objected that the holding of this office was inconsistent with his duties as preceptor of the King's grandchildren. Louis replied that he could live at

Court only for three months in the year, and during the other nine direct the studies of his pupils from Cambray.

Bossuet took part in the consecration of his friend Fénelon as Archbishop of Cambray; but after a time division of opinion arose. Jeanne Marie Bouvier de la Mothe Guyon became in 1676 a widow at the age of twenty-eight, with three children, for whose maintenance she gave up part of her fortune, and she then devoted herself to the practice and the preaching of a spiritual separation of the soul from earthly cares, and rest in God. She said with Galahad, "If I lose myself, I save myself." Her enthusiasm for a pure ideal, joined to her eloquence, affected many minds. It provoked opposition in the Church and in the Court, which was for the most part gross and self-seeking. Madame Guyon was attacked, even imprisoned. Fénelon felt the charm of her spiritual aspiration, and, without accepting its form, was her defender. Bossuet attacked her views. Fénelon published "Maxims of the Saints on the Interior Life." Bossuet wrote on "The States of Prayer." These were the rival books in a controversy about what was called "Quietism." Bossuet afterwards wrote a "Relation sur le Quietisme," of which Fénelon's copy, charged with his own marginal comments, is in the British Museum. In March, 1699, the Pope finally decided against Fénelon, and condemned his "Maxims of the Saints." Fénelon read from his pulpit the brief of condemnation, accepted the decision of the Pope, and presented to his church a piece of gold plate, on which the Angel of Truth was represented trampling many errors under foot, and among them his own "Maxims of the Saints." At Court, Fénelon was out of favour. "Télémaque," written for the young Duke of Burgundy, had not been published; but a copy having been obtained through a servant, it was printed, and its ideal of a true king and a true Court was so unlike his Majesty Louis XIV. and the Court of France, and the image of what ought not to be was so like what was, that it was resented as a libel. "Télémaque" was publicly condemned; Fénelon was banished from Court, and restrained within the limits of his diocese. Though separated from his pupil, the young Duke of Burgundy (who died in 1712), Fénelon retained his pupil's warm affection. The last years of his own life Fénelon gave to his work in Cambray, until his death on the 7th of January, 1715. He wrote many works, of which this is one, and they have been collected into twenty volumes. The translation here given was anonymous, and was first published in the year 1713.

SECTION I. Metaphysical Proofs of the Existence of God are not within Everybody's reach.

I cannot open my eyes without admiring the art that shines throughout all nature; the least cast suffices to make me perceive the Hand that makes everything.

Men accustomed to meditate upon metaphysical truths, and to trace up things to their first principles, may know the Deity by its idea; and I own that is a sure way to arrive at the source of all truth. But the more direct and short that way is, the more difficult and unpassable it is for the generality of mankind who depend on their senses and imagination.

An ideal demonstration is so simple, that through its very simplicity it escapes those minds that are incapable of operations purely intellectual. In short, the more perfect is the way to find the First Being, the fewer men there are that are capable to follow it.

SECT. II. Moral Proofs of the Existence of God are fitted to every man's capacity.

But there is a less perfect way, level to the meanest capacity. Men the least exercised in reasoning, and the most tenacious of the prejudices of the senses, may yet with one look discover Him who has drawn Himself in all His works. The wisdom and power He has stamped upon everything He has made are seen, as it were, in a glass by those that cannot contemplate Him in His own idea. This is a sensible and popular philosophy, of which any man free from passion and prejudice is capable. Humana autem anima rationalis est, quæ mortalibus peccati pœna tenebatur, ad hoc diminutionis redacta ut per conjecturas rerum visibilium ad intelligenda invisibilia niteretur; that is, "The human soul is still rational, but in such a manner that, being by the punishment of sin detained in the bonds of death, it is so far reduced that it can only endeavour to arrive at the knowledge of things invisible through the visible."

SECT. III. Why so few Persons are attentive to the Proofs Nature affords of the Existence of God.

If a great number of men of subtle and penetrating wit have not discovered God with one cast of the eye upon nature, it is not matter of wonder; for either the passions they have been tossed by have still rendered them incapable of any fixed reflection, or the false prejudices that result from passions have, like a thick cloud, interposed between their eyes and that noble spectacle. A man deeply concerned in an affair of great importance, that should take up all the attention of his mind, might pass several days in a room treating about his concerns without taking notice of the proportions of the chamber, the ornaments of the chimney, and the pictures about him, all which objects would continually be before his eyes, and yet none of them make any impression upon him. In this manner it is that men spend their lives; everything offers God to their sight, and yet they see it nowhere. "He was in the world, and the world was made by Him, and nevertheless the world did not know Him"—In mundo erat, et mundus per ipsum factus est, et mundus eum non cognovit. They pass away their lives without perceiving that sensible representation of the Deity. Such is the fascination of worldly trifles that obscures their eyes! Fascinatio nugacitatis obscurat bona. Nay, oftentimes they will not so much as open them, but rather affect to keep them shut, lest they should find Him they do not look for. In short, what ought to help most to open their eyes serves only to close them faster; I mean the constant duration and regularity of the motions which the Supreme Wisdom has put in the universe. St. Austin tells us those great wonders have been debased by being constantly renewed; and Tully speaks exactly in the same manner. "By seeing every day the same things, the mind grows familiar with them as well as the eyes. It neither admires nor inquires into the causes of effects that are ever seen to happen in the same manner, as if it were the novelty, and not the importance of the thing itself, that should excite us to such an inquiry." Sed assiduitate quotidiana et consuetudine oculorum assuescunt animi, neque admirantur neque requirunt rationes earum rerum, quas semper vident, perinde quasi novit as nos magis quam magnitudo rerum debeat ad exquirendas causas excitare.

SECT. IV. All Nature shows the Existence of its Maker.

But, after all, whole nature shows the infinite art of its Maker. When I speak of an art, I mean a collection of proper means chosen on purpose to arrive at a certain end; or, if you please, it is an order, a method, an industry, or a set design. Chance, on the contrary, is a blind and necessary cause, which neither sets in order nor chooses anything, and which has neither will nor understanding. Now I maintain that the universe bears the character and stamp of a cause infinitely powerful and industrious; and, at the same time, that chance (that is, the blind and fortuitous concourse of causes necessary and void of reason) cannot have formed this universe. To this purpose it is not amiss to call to mind the celebrated comparisons of the ancients.

SECT. V. Noble Comparisons proving that Nature shows the Existence of its Maker. First Comparison, drawn from Homer's "Iliad."

Who will believe that so perfect a poem as Homer's "Iliad" was not the product of the genius of a great poet, and that the letters of the alphabet, being confusedly jumbled and mixed, were by chance, as it were by the cast of a pair of dice, brought together in such an order as is necessary to describe, in verses full of harmony and variety, so many great events; to place and connect them so well together; to paint every object with all its most graceful, most noble, and most affecting attendants; in short, to make every person speak according to his character in so natural and so forcible a manner? Let people argue and subtilise upon the matter as much as they please, yet they never will persuade a man of sense that the "Iliad" was the mere result of chance. Cicero said the same in relation to Ennius's "Annals;" adding that chance could never make one single verse, much less a whole poem. How then can a man of sense be induced to believe, with respect to the universe, a work beyond contradiction more wonderful than the "Iliad," what his reason will never suffer him to believe in relation to that poem? Let us attend another comparison, which we owe to St. Gregory Nazianzenus.

SECT. VI. Second Comparison, drawn from the Sound of Instruments.

If we heard in a room, from behind a curtain, a soft and harmonious instrument, should we believe that chance, without the help of any human hand, could have formed such an instrument? Should we say that the strings of a violin, for instance, had of their own accord ranged and extended themselves on a wooden frame, whose several parts had glued themselves together to form a cavity with regular apertures? Should we maintain that the bow formed without art should be pushed by the wind to touch every string so variously, and with such nice justness? What rational man could seriously entertain a doubt whether a human hand touched such an instrument with so much harmony? Would he not cry out, "It is a masterly hand that plays upon it?" Let us proceed to inculcate the same truth.

SECT. VII. Third Comparison, drawn from a Statue.

If a man should find in a desert island a fine statue of marble, he would undoubtedly immediately say, "Sure, there have been men here formerly; I perceive the workmanship of a skilful statuary; I admire with what niceness he has proportioned all the limbs of this body, in order to give them so much beauty, gracefulness, majesty, life, tenderness, motion, and action!"

What would such a man answer if anybody should tell him, "That's your mistake; a statuary never carved that figure. It is made, I confess, with an excellent gusto, and according to the rules of perfection; but yet it is chance alone made it. Among so many pieces of marble there was one that formed itself of its own accord in this manner; the rains and winds have loosened it from the mountains; a violent storm has thrown it plumb upright on this pedestal, which had prepared itself to support it in this place. It is a perfect Apollo, like that of Belvedere; a Venus that equals that of the Medicis; an Hercules, like that of Farnese. You would think, it is true, that this figure walks, lives, thinks, and is just going to speak. But, however, it is not in the least beholden to art; and it is only a blind stroke of chance that has thus so well finished and placed it."

SECT. VIII. Fourth Comparison, drawn from a Picture.

If a man had before his eyes a fine picture, representing, for example, the passage of the Red Sea, with Moses, at whose voice the waters divide themselves, and rise like two walls to let the Israelites pass dryfoot through the deep, he would see, on the one side, that innumerable multitude of people, full of confidence and joy, lifting up their hands to heaven; and perceive, on the other side, King Pharaoh with the Egyptians frighted and confounded at the sight of the waves that join again to swallow them up. Now, in good earnest, who would be so bold as to affirm that a chambermaid, having by chance daubed that piece of cloth, the colours had of their own accord ranged themselves in order to produce that lively colouring, those various attitudes, those looks so well expressing different passions, that elegant disposition of so many figures without confusion, that decent plaiting of draperies, that management of lights, that degradation of colours, that exact perspective—in short, all that the noblest genius of a painter can invent? If there were no more in the case than a little foam at the mouth of a horse, I own, as the story goes, and which I readily allow without examining into it, that a stroke of a pencil thrown in a pet by a painter might once in many ages happen to express it well. But, at least, the painter must beforehand have, with design, chosen the most proper colours to represent that foam, in order to prepare them at the end of his pencil; and, therefore, it were only a little chance that had finished what art had begun. Besides, this work of art and chance together being only a little foam, a confused object, and so most proper to credit a stroke of chance— an object without form, that requires only a little whitish colour dropped from a pencil, without any exact figure or correction of design. What comparison is there between that foam with a whole design of a large continued history, in which the most fertile fancy and the boldest genius, supported by the perfect knowledge of rules, are scarce sufficient to perform what makes an excellent picture? I cannot prevail with myself to leave these instances without desiring the reader to observe that the most rational men are naturally extreme loath to think that beasts have no manner of understanding, and are mere machines. Now, whence proceeds such an invincible averseness to that opinion in so many men of sense? It is because they suppose, with reason, that motions so exact, and according to the rules of perfect mechanism, cannot be made without some industry; and that artless matter alone cannot perform what argues so much knowledge. Hence it appears that sound reason naturally concludes that matter alone cannot, either by the simple laws of motion, or by the capricious strokes of chance, make even animals that are mere machines. Those philosophers themselves, who will not allow beasts to have any reasoning faculty, cannot avoid acknowledging that what they suppose to be blind and artless in these machines is yet full of wisdom and art in the First Mover, who made their springs and regulated their movements. Thus the most opposite philosophers perfectly agree in acknowledging that matter and chance cannot, without the help of art, produce all we observe in animals.

SECT. IX. A Particular Examination of Nature.

After these comparisons, about which I only desire the reader to consult himself, without any argumentation, I think it is high time to enter into a detail of Nature. I do not pretend to penetrate through the whole; who is able to do it? Neither do I pretend to enter into any physical discussion. Such way of reasoning requires a certain deep knowledge, which abundance of men of wit and sense never acquired; and, therefore, I will offer nothing to them but the simple prospect of the face of Nature. I will entertain them with nothing but what everybody knows, and which requires only a little calm and serious attention.

SECT. X. Of the General Structure of the Universe.

Let us, in the first place, stop at the great object that first strikes our sight, I mean the general structure of the universe. Let us cast our eyes on this earth that bears us. Let us look on that vast arch of the skies that covers us; those immense regions of air, and depths of water that surround us; and those bright stars that light us. A man who lives without reflecting thinks only on the parts of matter that are near him, or have any relation to his wants. He only looks upon the earth as on the floor of his chamber, and on the sun that lights him in the daytime as on the candle that lights him in the night. His thoughts are confined within the place he inhabits. On the contrary, a man who is used to contemplate and reflect carries his looks further, and curiously considers the almost infinite abysses that surround him on all sides. A large kingdom appears then to him but a little corner of the earth; the earth itself is no more to his eyes than a point in the mass of the universe; and he admires to see himself placed in it, without knowing which way he came there.

SECT. XI. Of the Earth.

Who is it that hung and poised this motionless globe of the earth? Who laid its foundation? Nothing seems more vile and contemptible; for the meanest wretches tread it under foot; but yet it is in order to possess it that we part with the greatest treasures. If it were harder than it is, man could not open its bosom to cultivate it; and if it were less hard it could not bear them, and they would sink everywhere as they do in sand, or in a bog. It is from the inexhaustible bosom of the earth we draw what is most precious. That shapeless, vile, and rude mass assumes the most various forms; and yields alone, by turns, all the goods we can desire. That dirty soil transforms itself into a thousand fine objects that charm the eye. In the compass of one year it turns into branches, twigs, buds, leaves, blossoms, fruits, and seeds, in order, by those various shapes, to multiply its liberalities to mankind. Nothing exhausts the earth; the more we tear her bowels the more she is liberal. After so many ages, during which she has produced everything, she is not yet worn out. She feels no decay from old age, and her entrails still contain the same treasures. A thousand generations have passed away, and returned into her bosom. Everything grows old, she alone excepted: for she grows young again every year in the spring. She is never wanting to men; but foolish men are wanting to themselves in neglecting to cultivate her. It is through their laziness and extravagance they suffer brambles and briars to grow instead of grapes and corn. They contend for a good they let perish. The conquerors leave uncultivated the ground for the possession of which they have sacrificed the lives of so many thousand men, and have spent their own in hurry and trouble. Men have before them vast tracts of land uninhabited and uncultivated; and they turn mankind topsy-turvy for one nook of that neglected ground in dispute. The earth, if well cultivated, would feed a hundred times more men than now she does. Even the unevenness of ground which at first seems to be a defect turns either into ornament or profit. The mountains arose and the valleys descended to the place the Lord had appointed for them. Those different grounds have their particular advantages, according to the divers aspects of the sun. In those deep valleys grow fresh and tender grass to feed cattle. Next to them opens a vast champaign covered with a rich harvest. Here, hills rise like an amphitheatre, and are crowned with vineyards and fruit trees. There high mountains carry aloft their frozen brows to the very clouds, and the torrents that run down from them become the springs of rivers. The rocks that show their craggy tops bear up the earth of mountains just as the bones bear up the flesh in human bodies. That variety yields at once a ravishing prospect to the eye, and, at the same time, supplies the divers wants of man. There is no ground so barren but has some profitable property. Not only black and fertile soil but even clay and gravel recompense a man's toil.

Drained morasses become fruitful; sand for the most part only covers the surface of the earth; and when, the husbandman has the patience to dig deeper he finds a new ground that grows fertile as fast as it is turned and exposed to the rays of the sun.

There is scarce any spot of ground absolutely barren if a man do not grow weary of digging, and turning it to the enlivening sun, and if he require no more from it than it is proper to bear, amidst stones and rocks there is sometimes excellent pasture; and their cavities have veins, which, being penetrated by the piercing rays of the sun, furnish plants with most savoury juices for the feeding of herds and flocks. Even sea-coasts that seem to be the most sterile and wild yield sometimes either delicious fruits or most wholesome medicines that are wanting in the most fertile countries. Besides, it is the effect of a wise over-ruling providence that no land yields all that is useful to human life. For want invites men to commerce, in order to supply one another's necessities. It is therefore that want that is the natural tie of society between nations: otherwise all the people of the earth would be reduced to one sort of food and clothing; and nothing would invite them to know and visit one another.

SECT. XII. Of Plants.

All that the earth produces being corrupted, returns into her bosom, and becomes the source of a new production. Thus she resumes all she has given in order to give it again. Thus the corruption of plants, and the excrements of the animals she feeds, feed her, and improve her fertility. Thus, the more she gives the more she resumes; and she is never exhausted, provided they who cultivate her restore to her what she has given. Everything comes from her bosom, everything returns to it, and nothing is lost in it. Nay, all seeds multiply there. If, for instance, you trust the earth with some grains of corn, as they corrupt they germinate and spring; and that teeming parent restores with usury more ears than she had received grains. Dig into her entrails, you will find in them stone and marble for the most magnificent buildings. But who is it that has laid up so many treasures in her bosom, upon condition that they should continually produce themselves anew? Behold how many precious and useful metals; how many minerals designed for the conveniency of man!

Admire the plants that spring from the earth: they yield food for the healthy, and remedies for the sick. Their species and virtues are innumerable. They deck the earth, yield verdure, fragrant flowers, and delicious fruits. Do you see those vast forests that seem as old as the world? Those trees sink into the earth by their roots, as deep as their branches shoot up to the sky. Their roots defend them against the winds, and fetch up, as it were by subterranean pipes, all the juices destined to feed the trunk. The trunk itself is covered with a tough bark that shelters the tender wood from the injuries of the air. The branches distribute by several pipes the sap which the roots had gathered up in the trunk. In summer the boughs protect us with their shadow against the scorching rays of the sun. In winter, they feed the fire that preserves in us natural heat. Nor is burning the only use wood is fit for; it is a soft though solid and durable matter, to which the hand of man gives, with ease, all the forms he pleases for the greatest works of architecture and navigation. Moreover, fruit trees by bending their boughs towards the earth seem to offer their crop to man. The trees and plants, by letting their fruit or seed drop down, provide for a numerous posterity about them. The tenderest plant, the least of herbs and pulse are, in little, in a small seed, all that is displayed in the highest plants and largest tree. Earth that never changes produces all those alterations in her bosom.

SECT. XIII. Of Water.

Let us now behold what we call water. It is a liquid, clear, and transparent body. On the one hand it flows, slips, and runs away; and on the other it assumes all the forms of the bodies that surround it, having properly none of its own. If water were more rarefied, or thinner, it would be a kind of air; and so the whole surface of the earth would be dry and sterile. There would be none but volatiles; no living creature could swim; no fish could live; nor would there be any traffic by navigation. What industrious and sagacious hand has found means to thicken the water, by subtilising the air, and so well to distinguish those two sorts of fluid bodies? If water were somewhat more rarefied, it could no longer sustain those prodigious floating buildings, called ships. Bodies that have the least ponderosity would presently sink under water. Who is it that took care to frame so just a configuration of parts, and so exact a degree of motion, as to make water so fluid, so penetrating, so slippery, so incapable of any consistency: and yet so strong to bear, and so impetuous to carry off and waft away, the most unwieldy bodies? It is docile; man leads it about as a rider does a well-managed horse. He distributes it as he pleases; he raises it to the top of steep mountains, and makes use of its weight to let it fall, in order to rise again, as high as it was at first. But man who leads waters with such absolute command is in his turn led by them. Water is one of the greatest moving powers that man can employ to supply his defects in the most necessary arts, either through the smallness or weakness of his body. But the waters which, notwithstanding their fluidity, are such ponderous bodies, do nevertheless rise above our heads, and remain a long while hanging there. Do you see those clouds that fly, as it were, on the wings of the winds? If they should fall, on a sudden, in watery pillars, rapid like a torrent, they would drown and destroy everything where they should happen to fall, and the other grounds would remain dry. What hand keeps them in those pendulous reservatories, and permits them to fall only by drops as if they distilled through a gardener's watering-pot? Whence comes it that in some hot countries, where scarce any rain ever falls, the nightly dews are so plentiful that they supply the want of rain; and that in other countries, such as the banks of the Nile and Ganges, the regular inundation of rivers, at certain seasons of the year, never fails to make up what the inhabitants are deficient in for the watering of the ground? Can one imagine measures better concerted to render all countries fertile and fruitful?

Thus water quenches, not only the thirst of men, but likewise of arid lands: and He who gave us that fluid body has carefully distributed it throughout the earth, like pipes in a garden. The waters fall from the tops of mountains where their reservatories are placed. They gather into rivulets in the bottom of valleys. Rivers run in winding streams through vast tracts of land, the better to water them; and, at last, they precipitate themselves into the sea, in order to make it the centre of commerce for all nations. That ocean, which seems to be placed in the midst of lands, to make an eternal separation between them, is, on the contrary, the common rendezvous of all the people of the earth, who could not go by land from one end of the world to the other without infinite fatigue, tedious journeys, and numberless dangers. It is by that trackless road, across the bottomless deep, that the whole world shakes hands with the new; and that the new supplies the old with so many conveniences and riches. The waters, distributed with so much art, circulate in the earth, just as the blood does in a man's body. But besides this perpetual circulation of the water, there is besides the flux and reflux of the sea. Let us not inquire into the causes of so mysterious an effect. What is certain is that the tide carries, or brings us back to certain places, at precise hours. Who is it that makes it withdraw, and then come back with so much regularity? A little more or less motion in that fluid mass would disorder all nature; for a little more motion in a tide or flood would drown whole kingdoms. Who is it that knew how to take such exact measures in immense bodies? Who is it that knew so well how to keep a just medium between too much and too little? What hand has set to the sea the unmovable boundary it must respect through the series of all ages by telling it: There, thy proud waves shall come and break? But these waters so fluid become, on a sudden, during the winter, as hard as rocks. The summits of high mountains have, even at all times, ice and snow, which are the springs of rivers, and soaking pasture-grounds render them more fertile. Here waters are sweet to quench the thirst of man; there they are briny, and yield a salt that seasons our meat, and makes it incorruptible. In fine, if I lift up my eyes, I perceive in the clouds that fly above us a sort of hanging seas that serve to temper the air, break the fiery rays of the sun, and water the earth when it is too dry. What hand was able to hang over our heads those great reservatories of waters? What hand takes care never to let them fall but in moderate showers?

SECT. XIV. Of the Air.

After having considered the waters, let us now contemplate another mass yet of far greater extent. Do you see what is called air? It is a body so pure, so subtle, and so transparent, that the rays of the stars, seated at a distance almost infinite from us, pierce quite through it, without difficulty, and in an instant, to light our eyes. Had this fluid body been a little less subtle, it would either have intercepted the day from us, or at most would have left us but a duskish and confused light, just as when the air is filled with thick fogs. We live plunged in abysses of air, as fishes do in abysses of water. As the water, if it were subtilised, would become a kind of air, which would occasion the death of fishes, so the air would deprive us of breath if it should become more humid and thicker. In such a case we should drown in the waves of that thickened air, just as a terrestrial animal drowns in the sea. Who is it that has so nicely purified that air we breathe? If it were thicker it would stifle us; and if it were too subtle it would want that softness which continually feeds the vitals of man. We should be sensible everywhere of what we experience on the top of the highest mountains, where the air is so thin that it yields no sufficient moisture and nourishment for the lungs. But what invisible power raises and lays so suddenly the storms of that great fluid body, of which those of the sea are only consequences? From what treasury come forth the winds that purify the air, cool scorching heats, temper the sharpness of winter, and in an instant change the whole face of heaven? On the wings of those winds the clouds fly from one end of the horizon to the other. It is known that certain winds blow in certain seas, at some stated seasons. They continue a fixed time, and others succeed them, as it were on purpose, to render navigation both commodious and regular: so that if men are but as patient, and as punctual as the winds, they may, with ease, perform the longest voyages.

SECT. XV. Of Fire.

Do you see that fire that seems kindled in the stars, and spreads its light on all sides? Do you see that flame which certain mountains vomit up, and which the earth feeds with sulphur within its entrails? That same fire peaceably lurks in the veins of flints, and expects to break out, till the collision of another body excites it to shock cities and mountains. Man has found the way to kindle it, and apply it to all his uses, both to bend the hardest metals, and to feed with wood, even in the most frozen climes, a flame that serves him instead of the sun, when the sun removes from him. That subtle flame glides and penetrates into all seeds. It is, as it were, the soul of all living things; it consumes all that is impure, and renews what it has purified. Fire lends its force and activity to weak men. It blows up, on a sudden, buildings and rocks. But have we a mind to confine it to a more moderate use? It warms man, and makes all sorts of food fit for his eating. The ancients, in admiration of fire, believed it to be a celestial gift, which man had stolen from the gods.

SECT. XVI. Of Heaven.

It is time to lift up our eyes to heaven. What power has built over our heads so vast and so magnificent an arch? What a stupendous variety of admirable objects is here? It is, no doubt, to present us with a noble spectacle that an Omnipotent Hand has set before our eyes so great and so bright objects. It is in order to raise our admiration of heaven, says Tully, that God made man unlike the rest of animals. He stands upright, and lifts up his head, that he may be employed about the things that were above him. Sometimes we see a duskish azure sky, where the purest fires twinkle. Sometimes we behold, in a temperate heaven, the softest colours mixed with such variety as it is not in the power of painting to imitate. Sometimes we see clouds of all shapes and figures, and of all the brightest colours, which every moment shift that beautiful decoration by the finest accidents and various effects of light. What does the regular succession of day and night denote? For so many ages as are past the sun never failed serving men, who cannot live without it. Many thousand years are elapsed, and the dawn never once missed proclaiming the approach of the day. It always begins precisely at a certain moment and place. The sun, says the holy writ, knows where it shall set every day. By that means it lights, by turns, the two hemispheres, or sides of the earth, and visits all those for whom its beams are designed. The day is the time for society and labour; the night, wrapping up the earth with its shadow, ends, in its turn, all manner of fatigue and alleviates the toil of the day. It suspends and quiets all; and spreads silence and sleep everywhere. By refreshing the bodies it renews the spirits. Soon after day returns to summon again man to labour and revive all nature.

SECT. XVII. Of the Sun.

But besides the constant course by which the sun forms days and nights it makes us sensible of another, by which for the space of six months it approaches one of the poles, and at the end of those six months goes back with equal speed to visit the other pole. This excellent order makes one sun sufficient for the whole earth. If it were of a larger size at the same distance, it would set the whole globe on fire and the earth would be burnt to ashes; and if, at the same distance, it were lesser, the earth would be all over frozen and uninhabitable. Again, if in the same magnitude it were nearer us, it would set us in flames; and if more remote, we should not be able to live on the terrestrial globe for want of heat. What pair of compasses, whose circumference encircles both heaven and earth, has fixed such just dimensions? That star does no less befriend that part of the earth from which it removes, in order to temper it, than that it approaches to favour it with its beams. Its kind, beneficent aspect fertilises all it shines upon. This change produces that of the seasons, whose variety is so agreeable. The spring silences bleak frosty winds, brings forth blossoms and flowers, and promises fruits. The summer yields rich harvests. The autumn bestows the fruits promised by the spring. The winter, which is a kind of night wherein man refreshes and rests himself, lays up all the treasures of the earth in its centre with no other design but that the next spring may display them with all the graces of novelty. Thus nature, variously attired, yields so many fine prospects that she never gives man leisure to be disgusted with what he possesses.

But how is it possible for the course of the sun to be so regular? It appears that star is only a globe of most subtle flame. Now, what is it that keeps that flame, so restless and so impetuous, within the exact bounds of a perfect globe? What hand leads that flame in so strait a way and never suffers it to slip one side or other? That flame is held by nothing, and there is no body that can either guide it or keep it under; for it would soon consume whatever body it should be enclosed in. Whither is it going? Who has taught it incessantly and so regularly to turn in a space where it is free and unconstrained? Does it not circulate about us on purpose to serve us? Now if this flame does not turn, and if on the contrary it is our earth that turns, I would fain know how it comes to be so well placed in the centre of the universe, as it were the focus or the heart of all nature. I would fain know also how it comes to pass that a globe of so subtle matter never slips on any side in that immense space that surrounds it, and wherein it seems to stand with reason that all fluid bodies ought to yield to the impetuosity of that flame.

In fine, I would fain know how it comes to pass that the globe of the earth, which is so very hard, turns so regularly about that planet in a space where no solid body keeps it fast to regulate its course. Let men with the help of physics contrive the most ingenious reasons to explain this phenomenon; all their arguments, supposing them to be true, will become proofs of the Deity. The more the great spring that directs the machine of the universe is exact, simple, constant, certain, and productive of abundance of useful effects, the more it is plain that a most potent and most artful hand knew how to pitch upon the spring which is the most perfect of all.

SECT. XVIII. Of the Stars.

But let us once more view that immense arched roof where the stars shine, and which covers our heads like a canopy. If it be a solid vault, what architect built it? Who is it that has fixed so many great luminous bodies to certain places of that arch and at certain distances? Who is it that makes that vault turn so regularly about us? If on the contrary the skies are only immense spaces full of fluid bodies, like the air that surrounds us, how comes it to pass that so many solid bodies float in them without ever sinking or ever coming nearer one another? For all astronomical observations that have been made in so many ages not the least disorder or irregular motion has yet been discovered in the heavens. Will a fluid body range in such constant and regular order bodies that swim circularly within its sphere? But what does that almost innumerable multitude of stars mean? The profusion with which the hand of God has scattered them through His work shows nothing is difficult to His power. He has cast them about the skies as a magnificent prince either scatters money by handfuls or studs his clothes with precious stones. Let who will say, if he pleases, that the stars are as many worlds like the earth we inhabit; I grant it for one moment; but then, how potent and wise must He be who makes worlds as numberless as the grains of sand that cover the sea-shore, and who, without any trouble, for so many ages governs all these wandering worlds as a shepherd does a flock of sheep? If on the contrary they are only, as it were, lighted torches to shine in our eyes in this small globe called earth, how great is that power which nothing can fatigue, nothing can exhaust? What a profuse liberality it is to give man in this little corner of the universe so marvellous a spectacle!

But among those stars I perceive the moon, which seems to share with the sun the care and office of lighting us. She appears at set times with all the other stars, when the sun is obliged to go and carry back the day to the other hemisphere. Thus night itself, notwithstanding its darkness, has a light, duskish indeed, but soft and useful. That light is borrowed from the sun, though absent:

and thus everything is managed with such excellent art in the universe that a globe near the earth, and as dark as she of itself, serves, nevertheless, to send back to her, by reflection, the rays it receives from the sun; and that the sun lights by means of the moon the people that cannot see him while he must light others.

It may be said that the motion of the stars is settled and regulated by unchangeable laws. I suppose it is; but this very supposition proves what I labour to evince. Who is it that has given to all nature laws at once so constant and so wholesome, laws so very simple, that one is tempted to believe they establish themselves of their own accord, and so productive of beneficial and useful effects that one cannot avoid acknowledging a marvellous art in them? Whence proceeds the government of that universal machine which incessantly works for us without so much as our thinking upon it? To whom shall we ascribe the choice and gathering of so many deep and so well conceited springs, and of so many bodies, great and small, visible and invisible, which equally concur to serve us? The least atom of this machine that should happen to be out of order would unhinge all nature. For the springs and movements of a watch are not put together with so much art and niceness as those of the universe. What then must be a design so extensive, so coherent, so excellent, so beneficial? The necessity of those laws, instead of deterring me from inquiring into their author, does but heighten my curiosity and admiration. Certainly, it required a hand equally artful and powerful to put in His work an order equally simple and teeming, constant and useful. Wherefore I will not scruple to say with the Scripture, "Let every star haste to go whither the Lord sends it; and when He speaks let them answer with trembling, Here we are," Ecce adsumus.

SECT. XIX. Of Animals, Beasts, Fowl, Birds, Fishes, Reptiles, and Insects.

But let us turn our eyes towards animals, which still are more worthy of admiration than either the skies or stars. Their species are numberless. Some have but two feet, others four, others again a great many. Some walk; others crawl, or creep; others fly; others swim; others fly, walk, or swim, by turns. The wings of birds, and the fins of fishes, are like oars, that cut the waves either of air or water, and steer the floating body either of the bird, or fish, whose structure is like that of a ship. But the pinions of birds have feathers with a down, that swells in the air, and which would grow unwieldy in the water. And, on the contrary, the fins of fishes have sharp and dry points, which cut the water, without imbibing it, and which do not grow heavier by being wet. A sort of fowl that swim, such as swans, keep their wings and most of their feathers above water, both lest they should wet them and that they may serve them, as it were, for sails. They have the art to turn those feathers against the wind, and, in a manner, to tack, as ships do when the wind does not serve. Water-fowls, such as ducks, have at their feet large skins that stretch, somewhat like rackets, to keep them from sinking on the oozy and miry banks of rivers.

Amongst the animals, wild beasts, such as lions, have their biggest muscles about the shoulders, thighs, and legs; and therefore these animals are nimble, brisk, nervous, and ready to rush forward. Their jaw-bones are prodigiously large, in proportion to the rest of their bodies. They have teeth and claws, which serve them, as terrible weapons, to tear in pieces and devour other animals. For the same reason, birds of prey, such as eagles, have a beak and pounces that pierce everything. The muscles of their pinions are extreme large and brawny, that their wings may have a stronger and more rapid motion: and so those creatures, though somewhat heavy, soar aloft and tower up easily to the very clouds, from whence they shoot, like a thunderbolt, on the quarry they have in view. Other animals have horns. The greatest strength of some lies in their backs and necks; and others can only kick. Every species, however, has both offensive and defensive arms. Their hunting is a kind of war, which they wage one against another, for the necessities of life. They have also laws and a government among themselves. Some, like tortoises, carry the house wherein they were born; others build theirs, as birds do, on the highest branches of trees, to preserve their young from the insult of unwinged creatures, and they even lay their nests in the thickest boughs to hide them from their enemies. Another, such as the beaver, builds in the very bottom of a pond the sanctuary he prepares for himself, and knows how to cast up dikes around it, to preserve himself by the neighbouring inundation. Another, like a mole, has so pointed and so sharp a snout, that in one moment he pierces through the hardest ground in order to provide for himself a subterranean retreat. The cunning fox digs a kennel with two holes to go out and come in at, that he may not be either surprised or trapped by the huntsmen. The reptiles are of another make. They curl, wind, shrink, and stretch by the springs of their muscles; they creep, twist about, squeeze, and hold fast the bodies they meet in their way; and easily slide everywhere. Their organs are almost independent one on the other; so that they still live when they are cut into two. The long-legged birds, says Cicero, are also long-necked in proportion, that they may bring down their bill to the ground, and take up their food. It is the same with the camel; but the elephant, whose neck through its bigness would be too heavy if it were as long as that of the camel, was furnished with a trunk, which is a contexture of nerves and muscles, which he stretches, shrinks, winds, and turns every way, to seize on bodies, lift them up, or throw them off: for which reason the Latins called that trunk a hand.

Certain animals seem to be made on purpose for man. The dog is born to caress and fawn upon him; to obey and be under command; to give him an agreeable image of society, friendship, fidelity, and tenderness; to be true to his trust; eagerly to hunt down, course, and catch several other creatures, to leave them afterwards to man, without retaining any part of the quarry. The horse, and such other animals, are within the reach and power of man; to ease him of his labour, and to take upon them a thousand burdens. They are born to carry, to walk, to supply man's weakness, and to obey all his motions. Oxen are endowed with strength and patience, in order to draw the plough and till the ground. Cows yield streams of milk. Sheep have in their fleeces a superfluity which is not for them, and which still grows and renews, as it were to invite men to shear them every year. Even goats furnish man with a long hair, for which they have no use, and of which he makes stuffs to cover himself. The skins of some beasts supply men with the finest and best linings, in the countries that are most remote from the sun.

Thus the Author of nature has clothed beasts according to their necessities; and their spoils serve afterwards to clothe men, and keep them warm in those frozen climes. The living creatures that have little or no hair have a very thick and very hard skin, like scales; others have even scales that cover one another, as tiles on the top of a house, and which either open or shut, as it best suits with the living creature, either to extend itself or shrink. These skins and scales serve the necessities of men: and thus in nature, not only plants but animals also are made for our use. Wild beasts themselves either grow tame or, at least, are afraid of man. If all countries were peopled and governed as they ought to be, there would not be anywhere beasts should attack men. For no wild beasts would be found but in remote forests, and they would be preserved in order to exercise the courage, strength, and dexterity of mankind, by a sport that should represent war; so that there never would be any occasion for real wars among nations. But observe that living creatures that are noxious to man are the least teeming, and that the most useful multiply most. There are, beyond comparison, more oxen and sheep killed than bears or wolves; and nevertheless the number of bears and wolves is infinitely less than that of oxen and sheep still on earth. Observe likewise, with Cicero, that the females of every species have a number of teats proportioned to that of the young ones they generally bring forth. The more young they bear, with the more milk-springs has nature supplied them, to suckle them.

While sheep let their wool grow for our use, silk-worms, in emulation with each other, spin rich stuffs and spend themselves to bestow them upon us. They make of their cod a kind of tomb, and shutting up themselves in their own work, they are new-born under another figure, in order to perpetuate themselves. On the other hand, the bees carefully suck and gather the juice of odorous and fragrant flowers, in order to make their honey; and range it in such an order as may serve for a pattern to men. Several insects are transformed, sometimes into flies, sometimes into worms, or maggots. If one should think such insects useless, let him consider that what makes a part of the great spectacle of the universe, and contributes to its variety, is not altogether useless to sedate and contemplative men. What can be more noble, and more magnificent, than that great number of commonwealths of living creatures so well governed, and every species of which has a different frame from the other? Everything shows how much the skill and workmanship of the artificer surpasses the vile matter he has worked upon. Every living creature, nay even gnats, appear wonderful to me. If one finds them troublesome, he ought to consider that it is necessary that some anxiety and pain be mixed with man's conveniences: for if nothing should moderate his pleasures, and exercise his patience, he would either grow soft and effeminate, or forget himself.

SECT. XX. Admirable Order in which all the Bodies that make up the Universe are ranged.

Let us now consider the wonders that shine equally both in the largest and the smallest bodies. On the one side, I see the sun so many thousand times bigger than the earth; I see him circulating in a space, in comparison of which he is himself but a bright atom. I see other stars, perhaps still bigger than he, that roll in other regions, still farther distant from us. Beyond those regions, which escape all measure, I still confusedly perceive other stars, which can neither be counted nor distinguished. The earth, on which I stand, is but one point, in proportion to the whole, in which no bound can ever be found. The whole is so well put together, that not one single atom can be put out of its place without unhinging this immense machine; and it moves in such excellent order that its very motion perpetuates its variety and perfection. Sure it must be the hand of a being that does everything without any trouble that still keeps steady, and governs this great work for so many ages; and whose fingers play with the universe, to speak with the Scripture.

SECT. XXI. Wonders of the Infinitely Little.

On the other hand the work is no less to be admired in little than in great: for I find as well in little as in great a kind of infinite that astonishes me. It surpasses my imagination to find in a handworm, as one does in an elephant or whale, limbs perfectly well organised; a head, a body, legs, and feet, as distinct and as well formed as those of the biggest animals. There are in every part of those living atoms, muscles, nerves, veins, arteries, blood; and in that blood ramous particles and humours; in these humours some drops that are themselves composed of several particles: nor can one ever stop in the discussion of this infinite composition of so infinite a whole.

The microscope discovers to us in every object as it were a thousand other objects that had escaped our notice. But how many other objects are there in every object discovered by the microscope which the microscope itself cannot discover? What should not we see if we could still subtilise and improve more and more the instruments that help out weak and dull sight? Let us supply by our imagination what our eyes are defective in; and let our fancy itself be a kind of microscope, and represent to us in every atom a thousand new and invisible worlds: but it will never be able incessantly to paint to us new discoveries in little bodies; it will be tired, and forced at last to stop, and sink, leaving in the smallest organ of a body a thousand wonders undiscovered.

SECT. XXII. Of the Structure or Frame of the Animal.

Let us confine ourselves within the animal's machine, which has three things that never can be too much admired: First, it has in it wherewithal to defend itself against those that attack it, in order to destroy it. Secondly, it has a faculty of reviving itself by food. Thirdly, it has wherewithal to perpetuate its species by generation. Let us bestow some considerations on these three things.

SECT. XXIII. Of the Instinct of the Animal.

Animals are endowed with what is called instinct, both to approach useful and beneficial objects, and to avoid such as may be noxious and destructive to them. Let us not inquire wherein this instinct consists, but content ourselves with matter of fact, without reasoning upon it.

The tender lamb smells his dam afar off, and runs to meet her. A sheep is seized with horror at the approach of a wolf, and flies away before he can discern him. The hound is almost infallible in finding out a stag, a buck, or a hare, only by the scent. There is in every animal an impetuous spring, which, on a sudden, gathers all the spirits; distends all the nerves; renders all the joints more supple and pliant; and increases in an incredible manner, upon sudden dangers, his strength, agility, speed, and cunning, in order to make him avoid the object that threatens his destruction. The question in this place is not to know whether beasts are endowed with reason or understanding; for I do not pretend to engage in any philosophical inquiry. The motions I speak of are entirely indeliberate, even in the machine of man. If, for instance, a man that dances on a rope should, at that time, reason on the laws and rules of equilibrium, his reasoning would make him lose that very equilibrium which he preserves admirably well without arguing upon the matter, and reason would then be of no other use to him but to throw him on the ground. The same happens with beasts; nor will it avail anything to object that they reason as well as men, for this objection does not in the least weaken my proof; and their reasoning can never serve to account for the motions we admire most in them. Will any one affirm that they know the nicest rules of mechanics, which they observe with perfect exactness, whenever they are to run, leap, swim, hide themselves, double, use shifts to avoid pursuing hounds, or to make use of the strongest part of their bodies to defend themselves? Will he say that they naturally understand the mathematics which men are ignorant of? Will he dare to advance that they perform with deliberation and knowledge all those impetuous and yet so exact motions which even men perform without study or premeditation? Will he allow them to make use of reason in those motions, wherein it is certain man does not? It is an instinct, will he say, that beasts are governed by. I grant it: for it is, indeed, an instinct. But this instinct is an admirable sagacity and dexterity, not in the beasts, who neither do, nor can then, have time to reason, but in the superior wisdom that governs them. That instinct, or wisdom, that thinks and watches for beasts, in indeliberate things, wherein they could neither watch nor think, even supposing them to be as reasonable as we, can be no other than the wisdom of the Artificer that made these machines. Let us therefore talk no more of instinct or nature, which are but fine empty names in the mouth of the generality that pronounce them. There is in what they call nature and instinct a superior art and contrivance, of which human invention is but a shadow. What is beyond all question is, that there are in beasts a prodigious number of motions entirely indeliberate, and which yet are performed according to the nicest rules of mechanics. It is the machine alone that follows those rules: which is a fact independent from all philosophy; and matter of fact is ever decisive. What would a man think of a watch that should fly or slip away, turn, again, or defend itself, for its own preservation, if he went about to break it? Would he not admire the skill of the artificer? Could he be induced to believe that the springs of that watch had formed, proportioned, ranged, and united themselves, by mere chance? Could he imagine that he had clearly explained and accounted for such industrious and skilful operation by talking of the nature and instinct of a watch that should exactly show the hour to his master, and slip away from such as should go about to break its springs to pieces?

SECT. XXIV. Of Food.

What is more noble than a machine which continually repairs and renews itself? The animal, stinted to his own strength, is soon tired and exhausted by labour; but the more he takes pains, the more he finds himself pressed to make himself amends for his labour, by more plentiful feeding. Aliments daily restore the strength he had lost. He puts into his body another substance that becomes his own, by a kind of metamorphosis. At first it is pounded, and being changed into a liquor, it purifies, as if it were strained through a sieve, in order to separate anything that is gross from it; afterwards it arrives at the centre, or focus of the spirits, where it is subtilised, and becomes blood. And running at last, and penetrating through numberless vessels to moisten all the members, it filtrates in the flesh, and becomes itself flesh. So many aliments, and liquors of various colours, are then no more than one and the same flesh; and food which was but an inanimate body preserves the life of the animal, and becomes part of the animal himself; the other parts of which he was composed being exhaled by an insensible and continual transpiration. The matter which, for instance, was four years ago such a horse, is now but air, or dung. What was then either hay, or oats, is become that same horse, so fiery and vigorous—at least, he is accounted the same horse, notwithstanding this insensible change of his substance.

SECT. XXV. Of Sleep.

The natural attendant of food is sleep; in which the animal forbears not only all his outward motions, but also all the principal inward operations which might too much stir and dissipate the spirits. He only retains respiration, and digestion; so that all motions that might wear out his strength are suspended, and all such as are proper to recruit and renew it go on freely of themselves. This repose, which is a kind of enchantment, returns every night, while darkness interrupts and hinders labour. Now, who is it that contrived such a suspension? Who is it that so well chose the operations that ought to continue; and, with so just discernment, excluded all such as ought to be interrupted? The next day all past fatigue is gone and vanished. The animal works on, as if he had never worked before; and this reviving gives him a vivacity and vigour that invites him to new labour. Thus the nerves are still full of spirits, the flesh smooth, the skin whole, though one would think it should waste and tear; the living body of the animal soon wears out inanimate bodies, even the most solid that are about it; and yet does not wear out itself. The skin of a horse, for instance, wears out several saddles; and the flesh of a child, though very delicate and tender, wears out many clothes, whilst it daily grows stronger. If this renewing of spirits were perfect, it would be real immortality, and the gift of eternal youth. But the same being imperfect, the animal insensibly loses his strength, decays and grows old, because everything that is created ought to bear a mark of nothingness from which it was drawn; and have an end.

SECT. XXVI. Of Generation.

What is more admirable than the multiplication of animals? Look upon the individuals: no animal is immortal. Everything grows old, everything passes away, everything disappears, everything, in short, is annihilated. Look upon the species: everything subsists, everything is permanent and immutable, though in a constant vicissitude. Ever since there have been on earth men that have taken care to preserve the memory of events, no lions, tigers, wild boars, or bears, were ever known to form themselves by chance in caves or forests. Neither do we see any fortuitous productions of dogs or cats. Bulls and sheep are never born of themselves, either in stables, folds, or on pasture grounds. Every one of those animals owes his birth to a certain male and female of his species.

All those different species are preserved much the same in all ages. We do not find that for three thousand years past any one has perished or ceased; neither do we find that any one multiplies to such an excess as to be a nuisance or inconveniency to the rest. If the species of lions, bears, and tigers multiplied to a certain excessive degree, they would not only destroy the species of stags, bucks, sheep, goats, and bulls, but even get the mastery over mankind, and unpeople the earth. Now who maintains so just a measure as never either to extinguish those different species, or never to suffer them to multiply too fast?

But this continual propagation of every species is a wonder with which we are grown too familiar. What would a man think of a watchmaker who should have the art to make watches, which, of themselves, should produce others ad infinitum in such a manner that two original watches should be sufficient to multiply and perpetuate their species over the whole earth? What would he say of an architect that should have the skill to build houses, which should build others, to renew the habitations of men, before the first should decay and be ready to fall to the ground? It is, however, what we daily see among animals. They are no more, if you please, than mere machines, as watches are. But, after all, the Author of these machines has endowed them with a faculty to reproduce or perpetuate themselves ad infinitum by the conjunction of both sexes. Affirm, if you please, that this generation of animals is performed either by moulds or by an express configuration of every individual; which of these two opinions you think fit to pitch upon, it comes all to one; nor is the skill of the Artificer less conspicuous. If you suppose that at every generation the individual, without being cast into a mould, receives a configuration made on purpose, I ask, who it is that manages and directs the configuration of so compounded a machine, and which argues so much art and industry? If, on the contrary, to avoid acknowledging any art in the case you suppose that everything is determined by the moulds, I go back to the moulds themselves, and ask, who is it that prepared them? In my opinion they are still greater matter of wonder than the very machines which are pretended to come out of them.

Therefore let who will suppose that there were moulds in the animals that lived four thousand years ago, and affirm, if he pleases, that those moulds were so inclosed one within another ad infinitum, that there was a sufficient number for all the generations of those four thousand years; and that there is still a sufficient number ready prepared for the formation of all the animals that shall preserve their species in all succeeding ages. Now, these moulds, which, as I have observed, must have all the configuration of the animal, are as difficult to be explained or accounted for as the animals themselves, and are besides attended with far more unexplicable wonders. It is certain that the configuration of every individual animal requires no more art and power than is necessary to frame all the springs that make up that machine; but when a man supposes moulds: first, he must affirm that every mould contains in little, with unconceivable niceness, all the springs of the machine itself. Now, it is beyond dispute that there is more art in making so compound a work in little than in a larger bulk. Secondly, he must suppose that every mould, which is an individual prepared for a first generation, contains distinctly within itself other moulds contained within one another ad infinitum, for all possible generations, in all succeeding ages. Now what can be more artful and more wonderful in matter of mechanism than such a preparation of an infinite number of individuals, all formed beforehand in one from which they are to spring? Therefore the moulds are of no use to explain the generations of animals without supposing any art or skill. For, on the contrary, moulds would argue a more artificial mechanism and more wonderful composition.

What is manifest and indisputable, independently from all the systems of philosophers, is that the fortuitous concourse of atoms never produces, without generation, in any part of the earth, any lions, tigers, bears, elephants, stags, bulls, sheep, cats, dogs, or horses. These and the like are never produced but by the encounter of two of their kind of different sex. The two animals that produce a third are not the true authors of the art that shines in the composition of the animal engendered by them. They are so far from knowing how to perform that art, that they do not so much as know the composition or frame of the work that results from their generation. Nay, they know not so much as any particular spring of it; having been no more than blind and unvoluntary instruments, made use of for the performance of a marvellous art, to which they are absolute strangers, and of which they are perfectly ignorant. Now I would fain know whence comes that art, which is none of theirs? What power and wisdom knows how to employ, for the performance of works of so ingenious and intricate a design, instruments so uncapable to know what they are doing, or to have any notion of it? Nor does it avail anything to suppose that beasts are endowed with reason. Let a man suppose them to be as rational as he pleases in other things, yet he must own, that in generation they have no share in the art that is conspicuous in the composition of the animals they produce.

Let us carry the thing further, and take for granted the most wonderful instances that are given of the skill and forecast of animals. Let us admire, as much as you please, the certainty with which a hound takes a spring into a third way, as soon as he finds by his nose that the game he pursues has left no scent in the other two. Let us admire the hind, who, they say, throws a good way off her young fawn, into some hidden place, that the hounds may not find him out by the scent of his strain. Let us even admire the spider who with her cobwebs lays subtle snares to trap flies, and fall unawares upon them before they can disentangle themselves. Let us also admire the hern, who, they say, puts his head under his wing, in order to hide his bill under his feathers, thereby to stick the breast of the bird of prey that stoops at him. Let us allow the truth of all these wonderful instances of rationality; for all nature is full of such prodigies. But what must we infer from them? In good earnest, if we carefully examine the matter, we shall find that they prove too much. Shall we say that animals are more rational than we? Their instinct has undoubtedly more certainty than our conjectures. They have learnt neither logic nor geometry, neither have they any course or method of improvement, or any science. Whatever they do is done of a sudden without study, preparation, or deliberation. We commit blunders and mistakes every hour of the day after we have a long while argued and consulted together; whereas animals, without any reasoning or premeditation, perform every hour what seems to require most discernment, choice, and exactness. Their instinct is in many things infallible; but that word instinct is but a fair name void of sense. For what can an instinct more just, exact, precise, and certain than reason itself mean but a more perfect reason? We must therefore suppose a wonderful reason and understanding either in the work or in the artificer; either in the machine or in him that made it. When, for instance, I find that a watch shows the hours with such exactness as surpasses my knowledge, I presently conclude that if the watch itself does not reason, it must have been made by an artificer who, in that particular, reasoned better and had more skill than myself. In like manner, when I see animals, who every moment perform actions that argue a more certain art and industry than I am master of, I immediately conclude that such marvellous art must necessarily be either in the machine or in the artificer that framed it. Is it in the animal himself? But how is it possible he should be so wise and so infallible in some things? And if this art is not in him, it must of necessity be in the Supreme Artificer that made that piece of work, just as all the art of a watch is in the skill of the watchmaker.

SECT. XXVII. Though Beasts commit some Mistakes, yet their Instinct is, in many cases, Infallible.

Do not object to me that the instinct of beasts is in some things defective, and liable to error. It is no wonder beasts are not infallible in everything, but it is rather a wonder they are so in many cases. If they were infallible in everything, they should be endowed with a reason infinitely perfect; in short, they should be deities. In the works of an infinite Power there can be but a finite perfection, otherwise God should make creatures like or equal to Himself, which is impossible. He therefore cannot place perfection, nor consequently reason, in his works, without some bounds and restrictions. But those bounds do not prove that the work is void of order or reason. Because I mistake sometimes, it does not follow that I have no reason at all, and that I do everything by mere chance, but only that my reason is stinted and imperfect. In like manner, because a beast is not by his instinct infallible in everything, though he be so in many, it does not follow that there is no manner of reason in that machine, but only that such a machine has not a boundless reason. But, after all, it is a constant truth that in the operations of that machine there is a regular conduct, a marvellous art, and a skill which in many cases amounts to infallibility. Now, to whom shall we ascribe this infallible skill? To the work, or its Artificer?

SECT. XXVIII. It is impossible Beasts should have Souls.

If you affirm that beasts have souls different from their machines, I immediately ask you, "Of what nature are those souls entirely different from and united to bodies? Who is it that knew how to unite them to natures so vastly different? Who is it that has such absolute command over so opposite natures, as to put and keep them in such a regular and constant a society, and wherein mutual agreement and correspondence are so necessary and so quick?

If, on the contrary, you suppose that the same matter may sometimes think, and sometimes not think, according to the various wrangling and configurations it may receive, I will not tell you in this place that matter cannot think; and that one cannot conceive that the parts of a stone, without adding anything to it, may ever know themselves, whatever degree of motion, whatever figure, you may give them. I will only ask you now wherein that precise ranging and configuration of parts, which you speak of, consists? According to your opinion there must be a degree of motion wherein matter does not yet reason, and then another much like it wherein, on a sudden, it begins to reason and know itself. Now, who is it that knew how to pitch upon that precise degree of motion? Who is it that has discovered the line in which the parts ought to move? Who is it that has measured the dimensions so nicely as to find out and state the bigness and figure every part must have to keep all manner of proportions between themselves in the whole? Who is it that has regulated the outward form by which all those bodies are to be stinted? In a word, who is it that has found all the combinations wherein matter thinks, and without the least of which matter must immediately cease to think? If you say it is chance, I answer that you make chance rational to such a degree as to be the source of reason itself. Strange prejudice and intoxication of some men, not to acknowledge a most intelligent cause, from which we derive all intelligence; and rather choose to affirm that the purest reason is but the effect of the blindest of all causes in such a subject as matter, which of itself is altogether incapable of knowledge! Certainly there is nothing a man of sense would not admit rather than so extravagant and absurd an opinion.

SECT. XXIX. Sentiments of some of the Ancients concerning the Soul and Knowledge of Beasts.

The philosophy of the ancients, though very lame and imperfect, had nevertheless a glimpse of this difficulty; and, therefore, in order to remove it, some of them pretended that the Divine Spirit interspersed and scattered throughout the universe is a superior Wisdom that continually operates in all nature, especially in animals, just as souls act in bodies; and that this continual impression or impulse of the Divine Spirit, which the vulgar call instinct, without knowing the true signification of that word, was the life of all living creatures. They added, "That those sparks of the Divine Spirit were the principle of all generations; that animals received them in their conception and at their birth; and that the moment they died those divine particles disengaged themselves from all terrestrial matter in order to fly up to heaven, where they shone and rolled among the stars. It is this philosophy, at once so magnificent and so fabulous, which Virgil so gracefully expresses in the following verses upon bees:—

"Esse apibus partem divinæ mentis, et haustus
Ætherios dixere: Deum namque ire per omnes
Terrasque, tractusque maris, cælumque profundum.
Hinc pecudes, armenta viros, genus omne ferarum,
Quemque sibi tenues nascentem arcessere vitas.
Scilicet huc reddi deinde, ac resoluta referri
Omnia, nec morti esse locum, sed viva volare
Sideris in numerum, atque alto succedere cælo."

That is:—

"Induced by such examples, some have taught
That bees have portions of ethereal thought,
Endued with particles of heavenly fires,

For God the whole created mass inspires.
Through heaven, and earth, and ocean depth He throws
His influence round, and kindles as He goes.
Hence flocks, and herds, and men, and beasts, and fowls,
With breath are quickened, and attract their souls.
Hence take the forms His prescience did ordain,
And into Him, at length, resolve again.
No room is left for death: they mount the sky,
And to their own congenial planets fly."

Dryden's "Virgil."

That Divine Wisdom that moves all the known parts of the world had made so deep an impression upon the Stoics, and on Plato before them, that they believed the whole world to be an animal, but a rational and wise animal—in short, the Supreme God. This philosophy reduced Polytheism, or the multitude of gods, to Deism, or one God, and that one God to Nature, which according to them was eternal, infallible, intelligent, omnipotent, and divine. Thus philosophers, by striving to keep from and rectify the notions of poets, dwindled again at last into poetical fancies, since they assigned, as the inventors of fables did, a life, an intelligence, an art, and a design to all the parts of the universe that appear most inanimate. Undoubtedly they were sensible of the wonderful art that is conspicuous in nature, and their only mistake lay in ascribing to the work the skill of the Artificer.

SECT. XXX. Of Man.

Let us not stop any longer with animals inferior to man. It is high time to consider and study the nature of man himself, in order to discover Him whose image he is said to bear. I know but two sorts of beings in all nature: those that are endowed with knowledge or reason, and those that are not Now man is a compound of these two modes of being. He has a body, as the most inanimate corporeal beings have; and he has a spirit, a mind, or a soul—that is, a thought whereby he knows himself, and perceives what is about him. If it be true that there is a First Being who has drawn or created all the rest from nothing, man is truly His image; for he has, like Him, in his nature all the real perfection that is to be found in those two various kinds or modes of being. But an image is but an image still, and can be but an adumbration or shadow of the true Perfect Being.

Let us begin to study man by the contemplation of his body. "I know not," said a mother to her children in the Holy Writ, "how you were formed in my womb." Nor is it, indeed, the wisdom of the parents that forms so compounded and so regular a work. They have no share in that wonderful art; let us therefore leave them, and trace it up higher.

SECT. XXXI. Of the Structure of Man's Body.

The body is made of clay; but let us admire the Hand that framed and polished it. The Artificer's Seal is stamped upon His work. He seems to have delighted in making a masterpiece with so vile a matter. Let us cast our eyes upon that body, in which the bones sustain the flesh that covers them. The nerves that are extended in it make up all its strength; and the muscles with which the sinews weave themselves, either by swelling or extending themselves, perform the most exact and regular motions. The bones are divided at certain distances, but they have joints, whereby they are set one within another, and are tied by nerves and tendons. Cicero admires, with reason, the excellent art with which the bones are knit together. For what is more supple for all various motions? And, on the other hand, what is more firm and durable? Even after a body is dead, and its parts are separated by corruption, we find that these joints and ligaments can hardly be destroyed. Thus this human machine or frame is either straight or crooked, stiff or supple, as we please. From the brain, which is the source of all the nerves, spring the spirits, which are so subtle that they escape the sight; and nevertheless so real, and of so great activity and force, that they perform all the motions of the machine, and make up all in strength. These spirits are in an instant conveyed to the very extremities of the members. Sometimes they flow gently and regularly, sometimes they move with impetuosity, as occasion requires; and they vary ad infinitum the postures, gestures, and other actions of the body.

SECT. XXXII. Of the Skin.

Let us consider the flesh. It is covered in certain places with a soft and tender skin, for the ornament of the body. If that skin, that renders the object so agreeable, and gives it so sweet a colour, were taken off, the same object would become ghastly, and create horror. In other places that same skin is harder and thicker, in order to resist the fatigue of those parts. As, for instance, how harder is the skin of the feet than that of the face? And that of the hinder part of the head than that of the forehead? That skin is all over full of holes like a sieve: but those holes, which are called pores, are imperceptible. Although sweat and other transpirations exhale through those pores, the blood never runs out that way. That skin has all the tenderness necessary to make it transparent, and give the face a lively, sweet, and graceful colour. If the skin were less close, and less smooth, the face would look bloody, and excoriated. Now, who is that knew how to temper and mix those colours with such nicety as to make a carnation which painters admire, but never can perfectly imitate?

SECT. XXXIII. Of Veins and Arteries.

There are in man's body numberless branches of blood-vessels. Some of them carry the blood from the centre to the extreme parts, and are called arteries. Through those various vessels runs the blood, a liquor soft and oily, and by this oiliness proper to retain the most subtle spirits, just as the most subtle and spirituous essences are preserved in gummy bodies. This blood moistens the flesh, as springs and rivers water the earth; and after it has filtrated in the flesh, it returns to its source, more slowly, and less full of spirits: but it renews, and is again subtilised in that source, in order to circulate without ceasing.

SECT. XXXIV. Of the Bones, and their Jointing.

Do you consider that excellent order and proportion of the limbs? The legs and thighs are great bones jointed one with another, and knit together by tendons. They are two sorts of pillars, equal and regular, erected to support the whole fabric. But those pillars fold; and the rotula of the knee is a bone of a circular figure, which is placed on purpose on the joint, in order to fill it up, and preserve it, when the bones fold, for the bending of the knee. Each column or pillar has its pedestal, which is composed of various inlaid parts, so well jointed together, that they can either bend, or keep stiff, as occasion requires. The pedestal, I mean the foot, turns, at a man's pleasure, under the pillar. In this foot we find nothing but nerves, tendons, and little bones closely knit, that this part may, at once, be either more supple or more firm, according to various occasions. Even the toes, with their articles and nails, serve to feel the ground a man walks on, to lean and stand with more dexterity and nimbleness, the better to preserve the equilibrium of the body, to rise, or to stoop. The two feet stretch forward, to keep the body from falling that way, when it stoops or bends. The two pillars are jointed together at the top, to bear up the rest of the body, but are still divided there in such a manner, that that joint affords man the conveniency of resting himself, by sitting on the two biggest muscles of the body.

The body of the structure is proportioned to the height of the pillars. It contains such parts as are necessary for life, and which consequently ought to be placed in the centre, and shut up in the securest place. Therefore two rows of ribs pretty close to one another, that come out of the backbone, as the branches of a tree do from its trunk, form a kind of hoop, to hide and shelter those noble and tender parts. But because the ribs could not entirely shut up that centre of the human body, without hindering the dilatation of the stomach and of the entrails, they form that hoop but to a certain place, below which they leave an empty space, that the inside may freely distend and stretch, both for respiration and feeding.

As for the backbone, all the works of man afford nothing so artfully and curiously wrought. It would be too stiff, and too frangible or brittle, if it were made of one single bone: and in such a case man could never bend or stoop. The author of this machine has prevented that inconveniency by forming vertebræ, which jointing one with another make up a whole, consisting of several pieces of bones, more strong than if it were of a single piece. This compound being sometimes supple and pliant, and sometimes stiff, stands either upright, or bends, in a moment, as a man pleases. All these vertebræ have in the middle a gutter or channel, that serves to convey a continuation of the substance of the brain to the extremities of the body, and with speed to send thither spirits through that pipe.

But who can forbear admiring the nature of the bones? They are very hard; and we see that even the corruption of all the rest of the body, after death, does not affect them. Nevertheless, they are full of numberless holes and cavities that make them lighter; and in the middle they are full of the marrow, or pith, that is to nourish them. They are bored exactly in those places through which the ligaments that knit them are to pass. Moreover, their extremities are bigger than the middle, and form, as it were, two semicircular heads, to make one bone turn more easily with another, that so the whole may fold and bend without trouble.

SECT. XXXV. Of the Organs.

Within the enclosure of the ribs are placed in order all the great organs such as serve to make a man breathe; such as digest the aliments; and such as make new blood. Respiration, or breathing, is necessary to temper inward heat, occasioned by the boiling of the blood, and by the impetuous course of the spirits. The air is a kind of food that nourishes the animal, and by means of which he renews himself every moment of his life. Nor is digestion less necessary to prepare sensible aliments towards their being changed into blood, which is a liquor apt to penetrate everywhere, and to thicken into flesh in the extreme parts, in order to repair in all the members what they lose continually both by transpiration and the waste of spirits. The lungs are like great covers, which being spongy, easily dilate and contract themselves, and as they incessantly take in and blow out a great deal of air, they form a kind of bellows that are in perpetual motion. The stomach has a dissolvent that causes hunger, and puts man in mind of his want of food. That dissolvent, which stimulates and pricks the stomach, does, by that very uneasiness, prepare for it a very lively pleasure, when its craving is satisfied by the aliments. Then man, with delight, fills his belly with strange matter, which would create horror in him if he could see it as soon as it has entered his stomach, and which even displeases him, when he sees it being already satisfied. The stomach is made in the figure of a bagpipe. There the aliments being dissolved by a quick coction, or digestion, are all confounded, and make up a soft liquor, which afterwards becomes a kind of milk, called chyle; and which being at last brought into the heart, receives there, through the plenty of spirits, the form, vivacity, and colour of blood. But while the purest juice of the aliments passes from the stomach into the pipes destined for the preparation of chyle and blood, the gross particles of the same aliments are separated, just as bran is from flour by a sieve; and they are dejected downwards to ease the body of them, through the most hidden passages, and the most remote from the organs of the senses, lest these be offended at them. Thus the wonders of this machine are so great and numerous, that we find some unfathomable, even in the most abject and mortifying functions of the body, which modesty will not allow to be more particularly explained.

SECT. XXXVI. Of the Inward Parts.

I own that the inward parts are not so agreeable to the sight as the outward; but then be pleased to observe they are not made to be seen. Nay, it was necessary according to art and design that they should not be discovered without horror, and that a man should not without violent reluctance go about to discover them by cutting open this machine in another man. It is this very horror that prepares compassion and humanity in the hearts of men when one sees another wounded or hurt. Add to this, with St. Austin, that there are in those inward parts a proportion, order, and mechanism which still please more an attentive, inquisitive mind than external beauty can please the eyes of the body. That inside of man—which is at once so ghastly and horrid and so wonderful and admirable—is exactly as it should be to denote dirt and clay wrought by a Divine hand, for we find in it both the frailty of the creature and the art of the Creator.

SECT. XXXVII. Of the Arms and their Use.

From the top of that precious fabric we have described hang the two arms, which are terminated by the hands, and which bear a perfect symmetry one with another. The arms are knit with the shoulders in such a manner that they have a free motion, in that joint. They are besides divided at the elbow and at the wrist that they may fold, bend, and turn with quickness. The arms are of a just length to reach all the parts of the body. They are nervous and full of muscles, that they may, as well as the back, be often in action and sustain the greatest fatigue of all the body. The hands are a contexture of nerves and little bones set one within another in such a manner that they have all the strength and suppleness necessary to feel the neighbouring bodies, to seize on them, hold them fast, throw them, draw them to one, push them off, disentangle them, and untie them one from another.

The fingers, the ends of which are armed with nails, are by the delicacy and variety of their motions contrived to exercise the most curious and marvellous arts. The arms and hands serve also, according as they are either extended, folded, or turned, to poise the body in such a manner as that it may stoop without any danger of falling. The whole machine has, besides, independently from all after-thoughts, a kind of spring that poises it on a sudden and makes it find the equilibrium in all its different postures and positions.

SECT. XXXVIII. Of the Neck and Head.

Above the body rises the neck, which is either firm or flexible at pleasure. Must a man bear a heavy burden on his head? This neck becomes as stiff as if it were made up of one single bone. Has he a mind to bow or turn his head? The neck bends every way as if all its bones were disjointed. This neck, a little raised above the shoulders, bears up with ease the head, which over-rules and governs the whole body. If it were less big it would bear no proportion with the rest of the machine; and if it were bigger it would not only be disproportioned and deformed, but, besides, its weight would both crush the neck and put man in danger of falling on the side it should lean a little too much. This head, fortified on all sides by very thick and very hard bones in order the better to preserve the precious treasure it encloses, is jointed with the vertebræ of the neck, and has a very quick communication with all the other parts of the body. It contains the brain, whose moist, soft, and spongy substance is made up of tender filaments or threads woven together; this is the centre of all the wonders we shall speak of afterwards. The skull is regularly perforated, or bored, with exact proportion, and symmetry, for, the two eyes, the two ears, the mouth, and the nostrils. There are nerves destined for sensations, that exercise and play in most of those pipes. The nose, which has no nerves for its sensation, has a cribriform, or spongy bone, to let odours pass on to the brain. Amongst the organs of these sensations the chief are double, to preserve to one side what the other might happen to be defective in by any accident. These two organs of the same sensation are symmetrically placed either on the forepart or on the sides, that man may use them with more ease to the right or to the left or right against him—that is to say, towards the places his joints direct his steps and all his actions. Besides, the flexibility of the neck makes all those organs turn in an instant which way soever he pleases. All the hinder part of the head, which is the least able to defend itself, is therefore the thickest. It is adorned with hair which at the same time serves to fortify the head against the injuries of the air; and, on the other hand, the hair likewise adorns the fore part of the head and renders the face more graceful. The face is the fore part of the head, wherein the principal sensations meet and centre with an order and proportion that render it very beautiful unless some accident or other happen to alter and impair so regular a piece of work. The two eyes are equal, being placed about the middle, on the two sides of the head, that they may, without trouble, discover afar off both on the right and left all strange objects, and that they may commodiously watch for the safety of all the parts of the body.

The exact symmetry with which they are placed is the ornament of the face; and He that made them has kindled in them I know not what celestial flame, the like of which all the rest of nature does not afford. These eyes are a sort of looking-glasses, wherein all the objects of the whole world are painted by turns and without confusion in the bottom of the retina that the thinking part of man may see them in those looking-glasses. But though we perceive all objects by a double organ, yet we never see the objects double, because the two nerves that are subservient to sight in our eyes are but two branches that unite in one pipe, as the two glasses of a pair of spectacles unite in the upper part that joins them together. The two eyes are adorned with two equal eyebrows, and, that they may open and close, they are wrapped up with lids edged with hair that defend so delicate a part.

SECT. XXXIX. Of the Forehead and Other Parts of the Face.

The forehead gives majesty and gracefulness to all the face, and serves to heighten all its features. Were it not for the nose, which is placed in the middle, the whole face would look flat and deformed, of which they are fully convinced who have happened to see men in whom that part of the face is mutilated. It is placed just above the mouth, that it may the more easily discern, by the odours, whatever is most proper to feed man. The two nostrils serve at once both for the respiration and smell. Look upon the lips: their lively colour, freshness, figure, seat, and proportion, with the other features, render the face most beautiful. The mouth, by the correspondence of its motions with those of the eyes, animates, gladdens, suddens, softens, or troubles the face, and by sensible marks expresses every passion. The lips not only open to receive food, but by their suppleness and the variety of their motions serve likewise to vary the sounds that form speech. When they open they discover a double row of teeth with which the mouth is adorned. These teeth are little bones set in order in the two jaw-bones, which have a spring to open and another to shut in such a manner that the teeth grind, like a mill, the aliments in order to prepare their digestion. But these aliments thus ground go down into the stomach, through a pipe different from that through which we breathe, and these two pipes, though so neighbouring, have nothing common.

SECT. XL. Of the Tongue and Teeth.

The tongue is a contexture of small muscles and nerves so very supple, that it winds and turns like a serpent, with unconceivable mobility and pliantness. It performs in the mouth the same office which either the fingers or the bow of a master of music perform on a musical instrument: for sometimes it strikes the teeth, sometimes the roof of the mouth. There is a pipe that goes into the inside of the neck, called throat, from the roof of the mouth to the breast, which is made up of cartilaginous rings nicely set one within another, and lined within with a very smooth membrane, in order to render the air that is pushed from the lungs more sonorous. On the side of the roof of the mouth the end of that pipe is opened like a flute, by a slit, that either extends, or contracts itself as is necessary to render the voice either big or slender, hollow or clear. But lest the aliments, which have their separate pipe, should slide into the windpipe I have been describing, there is a kind of valve that lies on the orifice of the organ of the voice, and playing like a drawbridge, lets the aliments freely pass through their proper channel, but never suffers the least particle or drop to fall into the slit of the windpipe. This sort of valve has a very free motion, and easily turns any way, so that by shaking on that half-opened orifice, it performs the softest modulations of the voice. This instance is sufficient to show, by-the-by, and without entering long-winded details of anatomy, what a marvellous art there is in the frame of the inward parts. And indeed the organ I have described is the most perfect of all musical instruments, nor have these any perfection, but so far as they imitate that.

SECT. XLI. Of the Smell, Taste, and Hearing.

Who were able to explain the niceness of the organs by which man discerns the numberless savours and odours of bodies? But how is it possible for so many different voices to strike at once my ear without confounding one another, and for those sounds to leave in me, after they have ceased to be, so lively and so distinct images of what they have been? How careful was the Artificer who made our bodies to give our eyes a moist, smooth, and sliding cover to close them; and why did He leave our ears open? Because, says Cicero, the eyes must be shut against the light in order to sleep; and, in the meantime, the ears ought to remain open in order to give us warning, and wake us by the report of noise, when we are in danger of being surprised. Who is it that, in an instant, imprints in my eye the heaven, the sea, and the earth, seated at almost an infinite distance? How can the faithful images of all the objects of the universe, from the sun to an atom, range themselves distinctly in so small an organ? Is not the substance of the brain, which preserves, in order, such lively representations of all the objects that have made an impression upon us ever since we were in the world, a most wonderful prodigy? Men admire with reason the invention of books, wherein the history of so many events, and the collection of so many thoughts, are preserved. But what comparison can be made between the best book and the brain of a learned man? There is no doubt but such a brain is a collection infinitely more precious, and of a far more excellent contrivance, than a book. It is in that small repository that a man never misses finding the images he has occasion for. He calls them, and they come; he dismisses them, and they sink I know not where, and disappear, to make room for others. A man shuts or opens his fancy at pleasure, like a book. He turns, as it were, its leaves; and, in an instant, goes from one end to the other. There is even in memory a sort of table, like the index of a book, which shows where certain remote images are to be found. We do not find that these innumerable characters, which the mind of man reads inwardly with so much rapidity, leave any distinct trace or print in the brain, when we open it. That admirable book is but a soft substance, or a sort of bottom made up of tender threads, woven one with another. Now what skilful hand has laid up in that kind of dirt, which appears so shapeless, such precious images, ranged with such excellent and curious art?

SECT. XLII. Of the Proportion of Man's Body.

Such is the body of man in general: for I do not enter into an anatomical detail, my design being only to discover the art that is conspicuous in nature, by the simple cast of an eye, without any science. The body of man might undoubtedly be either much bigger and taller, or much lesser and smaller. But if, for instance, it were but one foot high, it would be insulted by most animals, that would tread and crush it under their feet. If it were as tall as a high steeple, a small number of men would in a few days consume all the aliments a whole country affords. They could find neither horses nor any other beasts of burden either to carry them on their backs or draw them in a machine with wheels; nor could they find sufficient quantity of materials to build houses proportioned to their bigness; and as there could be but a small number of men upon earth, so they should want most conveniences. Now, who is it that has so well regulated the size of man to so just a standard? Who is it that has fixed that of other animals and living creatures, with proportion to that of man? Of all animals, man only stands upright on his feet, which gives him a nobleness and majesty that distinguishes him, even as to the outside, from all that lives upon earth. Not only his figure is the noblest, but he is also the strongest and most dextrous of all animals, in proportion to his bigness. Let one nicely examine the bulk and weight of the most terrible beasts, and he will find, that though they have more matter than the body of a man, yet a vigorous man has more strength of body than most wild beasts. Nor are these dreadful to him, except in their teeth and claws. But man, who has not such natural arms in his limbs, has yet hands, whose dexterity to make artificial weapons surpasses all that nature has bestowed upon beasts. Thus man either pierces with his darts or draws into his snares, masters, and leads in chains the strongest and fiercest animals. Nay, he has the skill to tame them in their captivity, and to sport with them as he pleases. He teaches lions and tigers to caress him: and gets on the back of elephants.

SECT. XLIII. Of the Soul, which alone, among all Creatures, Thinks and Knows.

But the body of man, which appears to be the masterpiece of nature, is not to be compared to his thought. It is certain that there are bodies that do not think: man, for instance, ascribes no knowledge to stone, wood, or metals, which undoubtedly are bodies. Nay, it is so natural to believe that matter cannot think, that all unprejudiced men cannot forbear laughing when they hear any one assert that beasts are but mere machines; because they cannot conceive that mere machines can have such knowledge as they pretend to perceive in beasts. They think it to be like children's playing, and talking to their puppets, the ascribing any knowledge to mere machines. Hence it is that the ancients themselves, who knew no real substance but the body, pretended, however, that the soul of a man was a fifth element, or a sort of quintessence without name, unknown here below, indivisible, immutable, and altogether celestial and divine, because they could not conceive that the terrestrial matter of the four elements could think, and know itself: Aristoteles quintam quandam naturam censet esse, è quâ sit mens. Cogitare enim, et providere, et discere, et docere. . . . in horum quatuor generum nullo inesse putat; quintum genus adhibet vacans nomine.

SECT. XLIV. Matter Cannot Think.

But let us suppose whatever you please, for I will not enter the lists with any sect of philosophers: here is an alternative which no philosopher can avoid. Either matter can become a thinking substance, without adding anything to it, or matter cannot think at all, and so what thinks in us is a substance distinct from matter, and which is united to it. If matter can acquire the faculty of thinking without adding anything to it, it must, at least, be owned that all matter does not think, and that even some matter that now thinks did not think fifty years ago; as, for instance, the matter of which the body of a young man is made up did not think ten years before he was born. It must then be concluded that matter can acquire the faculty of thinking by a certain configuration, ranging, and motion of its parts. Let us, for instance, suppose the matter of a stone, or of a heap of sand. It is agreed this part of matter has no manner of thought; and therefore to make it begin to think, all its parts must be configurated, ranged, and moved a certain way and to a certain degree. Now, who is it that knew how to find, with so much niceness, that proportion, order, and motion that way, and to such a degree, above and below which matter would never think? Who is it that has given all those just, exact, and precise modifications to a vile and shapeless matter, in order to form the body of a child, and to render it rational by degrees? If, on the contrary, it be affirmed that matter cannot become a thinking substance without adding something to it, and that another being must be united to it, I ask, what will that other thinking being be, whilst the matter, to which it is united, only moves? Therefore, here are two natures or substances very unlike and distinct. We know one by figures and local motions only; as we do the other by perceptions and reasonings. The one does not imply, or create the idea of the other, for their respective ideas have nothing in common.

SECT. XLV. Of the Union of the Soul and Body, of which God alone can be the Author.

But now, how comes it to pass that beings so unlike are so intimately united together in man? Whence comes it that certain motions of the body so suddenly and so infallibly raise certain thoughts in the soul? Whence comes it that the thoughts of the soul, so suddenly and so infallibly, occasion certain motions in the body? Whence proceeds so regular a society, for seventy or fourscore years, without any interruption? How comes it to pass that this union of two beings, and two operations, so very different, make up so exact a compound, that many are tempted to believe it to be a simple and indivisible whole? What hand had the skill to unite and tie together these two extremes and opposites? It is certain they did not unite themselves by mutual consent, for matter having of itself neither thought nor will, to make terms and conditions, it could not enter into an agreement with the mind. On the other hand, the mind does not remember that it ever made an agreement with matter; nor could it be subjected to such an agreement, if it had quite forgot it. If the mind had freely, and of its own accord, resolved to submit to the impressions of matter, it would not, however, subject itself to them but when it should remember such a resolution, which, besides, it might alter at pleasure. Nevertheless, it is certain that in spite of itself it is dependent on the body, and that it cannot free itself from its dependence, unless it destroy the organs of the body by a violent death. Besides, although the mind had voluntarily subjected itself to matter, it would not follow that matter were reciprocally subjected to the mind. The mind would indeed have certain thoughts when the body should have certain motions, but the body would not be determined to have, in its turn, certain motions, as soon as the mind should have certain thoughts. Now it is most certain that this dependence is reciprocal. Nothing is more absolute than the command of the mind over the body. The mind wills, and, instantly, all the members of the body are in motion, as if they were acted by the most powerful machines. On the other hand, nothing is more manifest than the power and influence of the body over the mind. The body is in motion, and, instantly the mind is forced to think either with pleasure or pain, upon certain objects. Now, what hand equally powerful over these two divers and distinct natures has been able to bring them both under the same yoke, and hold them captive in so exact and inviolable a society? Will any man say it was chance? If he does, will he be able either to understand what he means, or to make it understood by others? Has chance, by a concourse of atoms, hooked together the parts of the body with the mind? If the mind can be hooked with some parts of the body, it must have parts itself, and consequently be a perfect body, in which case, we relapse into the first answer, which I have already confuted. If, on the contrary, the mind has no parts, nothing can hook it with those of the body, nor has chance wherewithal to tie them together.

In short, my alternative ever returns, and is peremptory and decisive. If the mind and body are a whole made up of matter only, how comes it to pass that this matter, which yesterday did not, has this day begun to think? Who is it that has bestowed upon it what it had not, and which is without comparison more noble than thoughtless matter? What bestows thought upon it, has it not itself, and how can it give what it has not? Let us even suppose that thought should result from a certain configuration, ranging, and degree of motion a certain way, of all the parts of matter: what artificer has had the skill to find out all those just, nice, and exact combinations, in order to make a thinking machine? If, on the contrary, the mind and body are two distinct natures, what power superior to those two natures has been able to unite and tie together without the mind's assent, or so much as its knowing which way that union was made? Who is it that with such absolute and supreme command over-rules both minds and bodies, and keeps them in society and correspondence, and under a sort of incomprehensible policy?

SECT. XLVI. The Soul has an Absolute Command over the Body.

Be pleased to observe that the command of my mind over my body is supreme and absolute in its bounded extent, since my single will, without any effort or preparation, causes all the members of my body to move on a sudden and immediately, according to the rules of mechanics. As the Scripture gives us the character of God, who said after the creation of the universe, "Let there be light, and there was light"—in like manner, the inward word of my soul alone, without any effort or preparation, makes what it says. I say, for instance, within myself, through that inward, simple, and momentaneous word, "Let my body move, and it moves." At the command of that simple and intimate will, all the parts of my body are at work. Immediately all nerves are distended, all the springs hasten to concur together, and the whole machine obeys, just as if every one of the most secret of those organs heard a supreme and omnipotent voice. This is certainly the most simple and most effectual power that can be conceived. All the other beings within our knowledge afford not the like instance of it, and this is precisely what men that are sensible and persuaded of a Deity ascribe to it in all the universe.

Shall I ascribe it to my feeble mind, or rather to the power it has over my body, which is so vastly different from it? Shall I believe that my will has that supreme command of its own nature, though in itself so weak and imperfect? But how comes it to pass that, among so many bodies, it has that power over no more than one? For no other body moves according to its desires. Now, who is it that gave over one body the power it had over no other? Will any man be again so bold as to ascribe this to chance?

SECT. XLVII. The Power of the Soul over the Body is not only Supreme or Absolute, but Blind at the same time.

But that power, which is so supreme and absolute, is blind at the same time. The most simple and ignorant peasant knows how to move his body as well as a philosopher the most skilled in anatomy. The mind of a peasant commands his nerves, muscles, and tendons, which he knows not, and which he never heard of. He finds them without knowing how to distinguish them, or knowing where they lie; he calls precisely upon such as he has occasion for, nor does he mistake one for the other. If a rope-dancer, for instance, does but will, the spirits instantly run with impetuousness, sometimes to certain nerves, sometimes to others—all which distend or slacken in due time. Ask him which of them he set a-going, and which way he begun to move them? He will not so much as understand what you mean. He is an absolute stranger to what he has done in all the inward springs of his machine. The lute-player, who is perfectly well acquainted with all the strings of his instrument, who sees them with his eyes, and touches them one after another with his fingers, yet mistakes them sometimes. But the soul that governs the machine of man's body moves all its springs in time, without seeing or discerning them, without being acquainted with their figure, situation, or strength, and yet it never mistakes. What prodigy is here! My mind commands what it knows not, and cannot see; what neither has, nor is capable of any knowledge. And yet it is infallibly obeyed. How much blindness and how much power at once is here! The blindness is man's; but the power, whose is it? To whom shall we ascribe it, unless it be to Him who sees what man does not see, and performs in him what passes his understanding? It is to no purpose my mind is willing to move the bodies that surround it, and which it knows very distinctly; for none of them stirs, and it has not power to move the least atom by its will. There is but one single body, which some superior Power must have made its property. With respect to this body, my mind is but willing, and all the springs of that machine, which are unknown to it, move in time and in concert to obey him. St. Augustin, who made these reflections, has expressed them excellently well. "The inward parts of our bodies," says he, "cannot be living but by our souls; but our souls animate them far more easily than they can know them. . . . The soul knows not the body which is subject to it. . . . It does not know why it does not move the nerves but when it pleases; and why, on the contrary, the pulsation of veins goes on without interruption, whether the mind will or no. It knows not which is the first part of the body it moves immediately, in order thereby to move all the rest. . . . It does not know why it feels in spite of itself, and moves the members only when it pleases. It is the mind does these things in the body. But how comes it to pass it neither knows what she does, nor in what manner it performs it? Those who learn, anatomy," continues that father, "are taught by others what passes within, and is performed by themselves. Why," says he, "do I know, without being taught, that there is in the sky, at a prodigious distance from me, a sun and stars; and why have I occasion for a master to learn where motion begins? . . . When I move my finger, I know not how what I perform within myself is performed. We are too far above, and cannot comprehend ourselves."

SECT. XLVIII. The Sovereignty of the Soul over the Body principally appears in the Images imprinted in the Brain.

It is certain we cannot sufficiently admire either the absolute power of the soul over corporeal organs which she knows not, or the continual use it makes of them without discerning them. That sovereignty principally appears with respect to the images imprinted in our brain. I know all the bodies of the universe that have made any impression on my senses for a great many years past. I have distinct images of them that represent them to me, insomuch that I believe I see them even when they exist no more. My brain is like a closet full of pictures, which should move and set themselves in order at the master's pleasure. Painters, with all their art and skill, never attain but an imperfect likeness; whereas the pictures I have in my head are so faithful, that it is by consulting them I perceive all the defects of those made by painters, and correct them within myself. Now, do these images, more like their original than the masterpieces of the art of painting, imprint themselves in my head without any art? Is my brain a book, all the characters of which have ranged themselves of their own accord? If there be any art in the case, it does not proceed from me. For I find within me that collection of images without having ever so much as thought either to imprint them, or set them in order. Moreover, all these images either appear or retire as I please, without any confusion. I call them back, and they return; I dismiss them, and they sink I know not where. They either assemble or separate, as I please. But I neither know where they lie, nor what they are. Nevertheless I find them always ready. The agitation of so many images, old and new, that revive, join, or separate, never disturbs a certain order that is amongst them. If some of them do not appear at the first summons, at least I am certain they are not far off. They may lurk in some deep corner, but I am not totally ignorant of them as I am of things I never knew; for, on the contrary, I know confusedly what I look for. If any other image offers itself in the room of that I called for, I immediately dismiss it, telling it, "It is not you I have occasion for." But, then, where lie objects half-forgotten? They are present within me, since I look for them there, and find them at last. Again, in what manner are they there, since I look for them a long while in vain? What becomes of them? "I am no more," says St. Augustin, "what I was when I had the thoughts I cannot find again. I know not," continues that father, "either how it comes to pass that I am thus withdrawn from and deprived of myself, or how I am afterwards brought back and restored to myself. I am, as it were, another man, and carried to another place, when I look for, and do not find, what I had trusted to my memory. In such a case we cannot reach, and are, in a manner, strangers remote from ourselves. Nor do we come at us but when we find what we are in quest of. But where is it we look for but within us? Or what is it we look for but ourselves? . . . So unfathomable a difficulty astonishes us!" I distinctly remember I have known what I do not know at present. I remember my very oblivion. I call to mind the pictures or images of every person in every period of life wherein I have seen them formerly, so that the same person passes several times in my head. At first, I see one a child, then a young, and afterwards an old, man. I place wrinkles in the same face in which, on the other side, I see the tender graces of infancy. I join what subsists no more with what is still, without confounding these extremes. I preserve I know not what, which, by turns, is all that I have seen since I came into the world. Out of this unknown store come all the perfumes, harmonies, tastes, degrees, and mixtures of colours; in short, all the figures that have passed through my senses, and which they have trusted to my brain. I revive when I please the joy I felt thirty years ago. It returns; but sometimes it is not the same it was formerly, and appears without rejoicing me. I remember I have been well pleased, and yet am not so while I have that remembrance. On the other hand, I renew past sorrows and troubles. They are present; for I distinctly perceive them such as they were formerly, and not the least part of their bitterness and lively sense escapes my memory. But yet they are no more the same; they are dulled, and neither trouble nor disquiet me. I perceive all their severity without feeling it; or, if I feel it, it is only by representation, which turns a former smart and racking pain into a kind of sport and diversion, for the image of past sorrows rejoices me. It is the same with pleasures: a virtuous mind is afflicted by the memory of its disorderly unlawful enjoyments. They are present, for they appear with all their softest and most flattering attendants; but they are no more themselves, and such joys return only to make us uneasy.

SECT. XLIX. Two Wonders of the Memory and Brain.

Here, therefore, are two wonders equally incomprehensible. The first, that my brain is a kind of book, that contains a number almost infinite of images, and characters ranged in an order I did not contrive, and of which chance could not be the author. For I never had the least thought either of writing anything in my brain, or to place in any order the images and characters I imprinted in it. I had no other thought but only to see the objects that struck my senses. Neither could chance make so marvellous a book: even all the art of man is too imperfect ever to reach so high a perfection, therefore what hand had the skill to compose it?

The second wonder I find in my brain, is to see that my mind reads with so much ease, whatever it pleases, in that inward book; and read even characters it does not know. I never saw the traces or figures imprinted in my brain, and even the substance of my brain itself, which is like the paper of that book, is altogether unknown to me. All those numberless characters transpose themselves, and afterwards resume their rank and place to obey my command. I have, as it were, a divine power over a work I am unacquainted with, and which is incapable of knowledge. That which understands nothing, understands my thought and performs it instantly. The thought of man has no power over bodies: I am sensible of it by running over all nature. There is but one single body which my bare will moves, as if it were a deity; and even moves the most subtle and nicest springs of it, without knowing them. Now, who is it that united my will to this body, and gave it so much power over it?

SECT. L. The Mind of Man is mixed with Greatness and Weakness. Its Greatness consists in two things. First, the Mind has the Idea of the Infinite.

Let us conclude these observations by a short reflection on the essence of our mind; in which I find an incomprehensible mixture of greatness and weakness. Its greatness is real: for it brings together the past and the present, without confusion; and by its reasoning penetrates into futurity. It has the idea both of bodies and spirits. Nay, it has the idea of the infinite: for it supposes and affirms all that belongs to it, and rejects and denies all that is not proper to it. If you say that the infinite is triangular, the mind will answer without hesitation, that what has no bounds can have no figure. If you desire it to assign the first of the units that make up an infinite number, it will readily answer, that there can be no beginning, end, or number in the infinite; because if one could find either a first or last unit in it, one might add some other unit to that, and consequently increase the number. Now a number cannot be infinite, when it is capable of some addition, and when a limit may be assigned to it, on the side where it may receive an increase.

SECT. LI. The Mind knows the Finite only by the Idea of the Infinite.

It is even in the infinite that my mind knows the finite. When we say a man is sick, we mean a man that has no health; and when we call a man weak, we mean one that has no strength. We know sickness, which is a privation of health, no other way but by representing to us health itself as a real good, of which such a man is deprived; and, in like manner, we only know weakness, by representing to us strength as a real advantage, which such a man is not master of. We know darkness, which is nothing real, only by denying, and consequently by conceiving daylight, which is most real, and most positive. In like manner we know the finite only by assigning it a bound, which is a mere negation of a greater extent; and consequently only the privation of the infinite. Now a man could never represent to himself the privation of the infinite, unless he conceived the infinite itself: just as he could not have a notion of sickness, unless he had an idea of health, of which it is only a privation. Now, whence comes that idea of the infinite in us?

SECT. LII. Secondly, the Ideas of the Mind are Universal, Eternal, and Immutable.

Oh! how great is the mind of man! He carries within him wherewithal to astonish, and infinitely to surpass himself: since his ideas are universal, eternal, and immutable. They are universal: for when I say it is impossible to be and not to be; the whole is bigger than a part of it; a line perfectly circular has no straight parts; between two points given the straight line is the shortest; the centre of a perfect circle is equally distant from all the points of the circumference; an equilateral triangle has no obtuse or right angle: all these truths admit of no exception. There never can be any being, line, circle, or triangle, but according to these rules. These axioms are of all times, or to speak more properly, they exist before all time, and will ever remain after any comprehensible duration. Let the universe be turned topsy-turvy, destroyed, and annihilated; and even let there be no mind to reason about beings, lines, circles, and triangles: yet it will ever be equally true in itself, that the same thing cannot at once be and not be; that a perfect circle can have no part of a straight line; that the centre of a perfect circle cannot be nearer one side of the circumference than the other. Men may, indeed, not think actually on these truths: and it might even happen that there should be neither universe nor any mind capable to reflect on these truths: but nevertheless they are still constant and certain in themselves although no mind should be acquainted with them; just as the rays of the sun would not cease being real, although all men should be blind, and no body have eyes to be sensible of their light. By affirming that two and two make four, says St. Augustin, man is not only certain that he speaks truth, but he cannot doubt that such a proposition was ever equally true, and must be so eternally. These ideas we carry within ourselves have no bounds, and cannot admit of any. It cannot be said that what I have affirmed about the centre of perfect circles is true only in relation to a certain number of circles; for that proposition is true, through evident necessity, with respect to all circles ad infinitum. These unbounded ideas can never be changed, altered, impaired, or defaced in us; for they make up the very essence of our reason. Whatever effort a man may make in his own mind, yet it is impossible for him ever to entertain a serious doubt about the truths which those ideas clearly represent to us. For instance, I never can seriously call in question, whether the whole is bigger than one of its parts; or whether the centre of a perfect circle is equally distant from all the points of the circumference. The idea of the infinite is in me like that of numbers, lines, circles, a whole, and a part. The changing our ideas would be, in effect, the annihilating reason itself. Let us judge and make an estimate of our greatness by the immutable infinite stamp within us, and which can never be defaced from our minds. But lest such a real greatness should dazzle and betray us, by flattering our vanity, let us hasten to cast our eyes on our weakness.

SECT. LIII. Weakness of Man's Mind.

That same mind that incessantly sees the infinite, and, through the rule of the infinite, all finite things, is likewise infinitely ignorant of all the objects that surround it. It is altogether ignorant of itself, and gropes about in an abyss of darkness. It neither knows what it is, nor how it is united with a body; nor which way it has so much command over all the springs of that body, which it knows not. It is ignorant of its own thoughts and wills. It knows not, with certainty, either what it believes or wills. It often fancies to believe and will, what it neither believes nor wills. It is liable to mistake, and its greatest excellence is to acknowledge it. To the error of its thoughts, it adds the disorder and irregularity of its will and desires; so that it is forced to groan in the consciousness and experience of its corruption. Such is the mind of man, weak, uncertain, stinted, full of errors. Now, who is it that put the idea of

The Existence Of God

the infinite, that is to say of perfection, in a subject so stinted and so full of imperfection? Did it give itself so sublime, and so pure an idea, which is itself a kind of infinite in imagery? What finite being distinct from it was able to give it what bears no proportion with what is limited within any bounds? Let us suppose the mind of man to be like a looking-glass, wherein the images of all the neighbouring bodies imprint themselves. Now what being was able to stamp within us the image of the infinite, if the infinite never existed? Who can put in a looking-glass the image of a chimerical object which is not in being, and which was never placed against the glass? This image of the infinite is not a confused collection of finite objects, which the mind may mistake for a true infinite. It is the true infinite of which we have the thought and idea. We know it so well, that we exactly distinguish it from whatever it is not; and that no subtilty can palm upon us any other object in its room. We are so well acquainted with it, that we reject from it any propriety that denotes the least bound or limit. In short, we know it so well, that it is in it alone we know all the rest, just as we know the night by the day, sickness by health. Now, once more, whence comes so great an image? Does it proceed from nothing? Can a stinted limited being imagine and invent the infinite, if there be no infinite at all? Our weak and short-sighted mind cannot of itself form that image, which, at this rate, should have no author. None of the outward objects can give us that image: for they can only give us the image of what they are, and they are limited and imperfect. Therefore, from whence shall we derive that distinct image which is unlike anything within us, and all we know here below, without us? Whence does it proceed? Where is that infinite we cannot comprehend, because it is really infinite: and which nevertheless we cannot mistake, because we distinguish it from anything that is inferior to it? Sure it must be somewhere, otherwise how could it imprint itself in our minds?

SECT. LIV. The Ideas of Man are the Immutable Rules of his Judgment.

But besides the idea of the infinite, I have yet universal and immutable notions, which are the rule and standard of all my judgments; insomuch that I cannot judge of anything but by consulting them; nor am I free to judge contrary to what they represent to me. My thoughts are so far from being able to correct or form that rule, that they are themselves corrected, in spite of myself, by that superior rule; and invincibly subjected to its decision. Whatever effort my mind can make, I can never be brought, as I observed before, to entertain a doubt whether two and two make four; whether the whole is bigger than one of its parts; or whether the centre of a perfect circle be equally distant from all the points of the circumference. I am not free to deny those propositions; and if I happen to deny those truths, or others much like them, there is in me something above myself, which forces me to return to the rule. That fixed and immutable rule is so inward and intimate, that I am tempted to take it for myself. But it is above me, since it corrects and rectifies me; gives me a distrust of myself, and makes me sensible of my impotency. It is something that inspires me every moment, provided I hearken to it, and I never err or mistake except when I am not attentive to it. What inspires me would for ever preserve me from error, if I were docile, and acted without precipitation; for that inward inspiration would teach me to judge aright of things within my reach, and about which I have occasion to form a judgment. As for others, it would teach me not to judge of them at all, which second lesson is no less important than the first. That inward rule is what I call my reason; but I speak of my reason without penetrating into the extent of those words, as I speak of nature and instinct, without knowing what those expressions mean.

SECT. LV. What Man's Reason is.

It is certain my reason is within me, for I must continually recollect myself to find it; but the superior reason that corrects me upon occasion, and which I consult, is none of mine, nor is it part of myself. That rule is perfect and immutable; whereas I am changeable and imperfect. When I err, it preserves its rectitude. When I am undeceived, it is not set right, for it never was otherwise; and still keeping to truth has the authority to call, and bring me back to it. It is an inward master that makes me either be silent or speak; believe, or doubt; acknowledge my errors, or confirm my judgment. I am instructed by hearkening to it; whereas I err and go astray when I hearken to myself. That Master is everywhere, and His voice is heard, from one end of the universe to the other, by all men as well as me. Whilst He corrects and rectifies me in France, He corrects and sets right other men in China, Japan, Mexico, and in Peru, by the same principles.

SECT. LVI. Reason is the Same in all Men, of all Ages and Countries.

Two men who never saw or heard of one another, and who never entertained any correspondence with any other man that could give them common notions, yet speak at two extremities of the earth, about a certain number of truths, as if they were in concert. It is infallibly known beforehand in one hemisphere, what will be answered in the other upon these truths. Men of all countries and of all ages, whatever their education may have been, find themselves invincibly subjected and obliged to think and speak in the same manner. The Master who incessantly teaches us makes all of us think the same way. Whenever we hastily judge, without hearkening to His voice, in diffidence of ourselves, we think and utter dreams full of extravagance. Thus what appears most to be part of ourselves, and our very essence, I mean our reason, is least our own, and what, on the contrary, ought to be accounted most borrowed. We continually receive a reason superior to us, as we incessantly breathe the air, which is a foreign body; or as we incessantly see all the objects near us by the light of the sun, whose rays are bodies foreign to our eyes. That superior reason overrules and governs, to a certain degree, with an absolute power all men, even the least rational, and makes them all ever agree, in spite of themselves, upon those points. It is she that makes a savage in Canada think about a great many things, just as the Greek and Roman philosophers did. It is she that made the Chinese geometricians find out much of the same truths with the Europeans, whilst those nations so very remote were unknown one to another. It is she that makes people in Japan conclude, as in France, that two and two make four; nor is it apprehended that any nation shall ever change their opinion about it. It is she that makes men think nowadays about certain points, just as men thought about the same four thousand years ago. It is she that gives uniform thoughts to the most jealous and jarring men, and the most irreconcilable among themselves. It is by her that men of all ages and countries are, as it were, chained about an immovable centre, and held in the bonds of amity by certain invariable rules, called first principles, notwithstanding the infinite variations of opinions that arise in them from their passion, avocations, and caprices, which over-rule all their other less-clear judgments. It is through her that men, as depraved as they are, have not yet presumed openly to bestow on vice the name of virtue, and that they are reduced to dissemble being just, sincere, moderate, benevolent, in order to gain one another's esteem. The most wicked and abandoned of men cannot be brought to esteem what they wish they could esteem, or to despise what they wish they could despise. It is not possible to force the eternal barrier of truth and justice. The inward master, called reason, intimately checks the attempt with absolute power, and knows how to set bounds to the most impudent folly of men. Though vice has for many ages reigned with unbridled licentiousness, virtue is still called virtue; and the most brutish and rash of her adversaries cannot yet deprive her of her name. Hence it is that vice, though triumphant in the world, is still obliged to disguise itself under the mask of hypocrisy or sham honesty, to gain the esteem it has not the confidence to expect, if it should go bare-faced. Thus, notwithstanding its impudence, it pays a forced homage to virtue, by endeavouring to adorn itself with her fairest outside in order to receive the honour and respect she commands from men. It is true virtuous men are exposed to censure; and they are, indeed, ever reprehensible in this life, through their natural imperfections; but yet the most vicious cannot totally efface in themselves the idea of true virtue. There never was yet any man upon earth that could prevail either with others, or himself, to allow, as a received maxim, that to be knavish, passionate, and mischievous, is more honourable than to be honest, moderate, good-natured, and benevolent.

SECT. LVII. Reason in Man is Independent of and above Him.

I have already evinced that the inward and universal master, at all times, and in all places, speaks the same truths. We are not that master: though it is true we often speak without, and higher than him. But then we mistake, stutter, and do not so much as understand ourselves. We are even afraid of being made sensible of our mistakes, and we shut up our ears, lest we should be humbled by his corrections. Certainly the man who is apprehensive of being corrected and reproved by that uncorruptible reason, and ever goes astray when he does not follow it, is not that perfect, universal, and immutable reason, that corrects him, in spite of himself. In all things we find, as it were, two principles within us. The one gives, the other receives; the one fails, or is defective; the other makes up; the one mistakes, the other rectifies; the one goes awry, through his inclination, the other sets him right. It was the mistaken and ill-understood experience of this that led the Marcionites and Manicheans into error. Every man is conscious within himself of a limited and inferior reason, that goes astray and errs, as soon as it gets loose from an entire subordination, and which mends its error no other way, but by returning under the yoke of another superior, universal, and immutable reason. Thus everything within us argues an inferior, limited, communicated, and borrowed reason, that wants every moment to be rectified by another. All men are rational by means of the same reason, that communicates itself to them, according to various degrees. There is a certain number of wise men; but the wisdom from which they draw theirs, as from an inexhaustible source, and which makes them what they are, is but ONE.

SECT. LVIII. It is the Primitive Truth, that Lights all Minds, by communicating itself to them.

Where is that wisdom? Where is that reason, at once both common and superior to all limited and imperfect reasons of mankind? Where is that oracle, which is never silent, and against which all the vain prejudices of men cannot prevail? Where is that reason which we have ever occasion to consult, and which prevents us to create in us the desire of hearing its voice? Where is that lively light which lighteth every man that cometh into the world? Where is that pure and soft light, which not only lights those eyes that are open, but which opens eyes that are shut; cures sore eyes; gives eyes to those that have none to see it; in short, which raises the desire of being lighted by it, and gains even their love, who were afraid to see it? Every eye sees it; nor would it see anything, unless it saw it; since it is by that light and its pure rays that the eye sees everything. As the sensibler sun in the firmament lights all bodies, so the sun of intelligence lights all minds. The substance of a man's eye is not the light: on the contrary, the eye borrows, every moment, the light from the rays of the sun. Just in the same manner, my mind is not the primitive reason, or universal and immutable truth; but only the organ through which that original light passes, and which is lighted by it. There is a sun of spirits that lights them far better than the visible sun lights bodies. This sun of spirits gives us, at once, both its light, and the love of it, in order to seek it. That sun of truth leaves no manner of darkness, and shines at the same time in the two hemispheres. It lights us as much by night as by day; nor does it spread its rays outwardly; but inhabits in every one of us. A man can never deprive another man of its beams. One sees it equally, in whatever corner of the universe he may lurk. A man never needs say to another, step aside, to let me see that sun; you rob me of its rays; you take away my share of it. That sun never sets: nor suffers any cloud, but such as are raised by our passions. It is a day without shadow. It lights the savages even in the deepest and darkest caves; none but sore eyes wink against its light; nor is there indeed any man so distempered and so blind, but who still walks by the glimpse of some duskish light he retains from that inward sun of consciences. That universal light discovers and represents all objects to our minds; nor can we judge of anything but by it; just as we cannot discern anybody but by the rays of the sun.

SECT. LIX. It is by the Light of Primitive Truth a Man Judges whether what one says to him be True or False.

Men may speak and discourse to us in order to instruct us: but we cannot believe them any farther, than we find a certain conformity or agreement between what they say, and what the inward master says. After they have exhausted all their arguments, we must still return, and hearken to him, for a final decision. If a man should tell us that a part equals the whole of which it is a part, we should not be able to forbear laughing, and instead of persuading us, he would make himself ridiculous to us. It is in the very bottom of ourselves, by consulting the inward master, that we must find the truths that are taught us, that is, which are outwardly proposed to us. Thus, properly speaking, there is but one true Master, who teaches all, and without whom one learns nothing. Other masters always refer and bring us back to that inward school where he alone speaks. It is there we receive what we have not; it is there we learn what we were ignorant of; and find what we had lost by oblivion. It is in the intimate bottom of ourselves, he keeps in store for us certain truths, that lie, as it were, buried, but which revive upon occasion; and it is there, in short, that we reject the falsehood we had embraced. Far from judging that master, it is by him alone we are judged peremptorily in all things. He is a judge disinterested, impartial, and superior to us. We may, indeed, refuse hearing him, and raise a din to stun our ears: but when we hear him it is not in our power to contradict him. Nothing is more unlike man than that invisible master that instructs and judges him with so much severity, uprightness, and perfection. Thus our limited, uncertain, defective, fallible reason, is but a feeble and momentaneous inspiration of a primitive, supreme, and immutable reason, which communicates itself with measure, to all intelligent beings.

SECT. LX. The Superior Reason that resides in Man is God Himself; and whatever has been above discovered to be in Man, are evident Footsteps of the Deity.

It cannot be said that man gives himself the thoughts he had not before; much less can it be said that he receives them from other men, since it is certain he neither does nor can admit anything from without, unless he finds it in his own bottom, by consulting within him the principles of reason, in order to examine whether what he is told is agreeable or repugnant to them. Therefore there is an inward school wherein man receives what he neither can give himself, nor expect from other men who live upon trust as well as himself. Here then, are two reasons I find within me; one of which, is myself, the other is above me. That which is myself is very imperfect, prejudiced, liable to error, changeable, headstrong, ignorant, and limited; in short it possesses nothing but what is borrowed. The other is common to all men, and superior to them. It is perfect, eternal, immutable, ever ready to communicate itself in all places, and to rectify all minds that err and mistake; in short, incapable of ever being either exhausted or divided, although it communicates itself to all who desire it. Where is that perfect reason which is so near me, and yet so different from me? Where is it? Sure it must be something real; for nothing or nought cannot either be perfect or make perfect imperfect natures. Where is that supreme reason? Is it not the very God I look for?

SECT. LXI. New sensible Notices of the Deity in Man, drawn from the Knowledge he has of Unity.

I still find other traces or notices of the Deity within me: here is a very sensible one. I am acquainted with prodigious numbers with the relations that are between them. Now how come I by that knowledge? It is so very distinct that I cannot seriously doubt of it; and so, immediately, without the least hesitation, I rectify any man that does not follow it in computation. If a man says seventeen and three make twenty-two, I presently tell him seventeen and three make but twenty; and he is immediately convinced by his own light, and acquiesces in my correction. The same Master who speaks within me to correct him speaks at the same time within him to bid him acquiesce. These are not two masters that have agreed to make us agree. It is something indivisible, eternal, immutable, that speaks at the same time with an invincible persuasion in us both. Once more, how come I by so just a notion of numbers? All numbers are but repeated units. Every number is but a compound, or a repetition of units. The number of two, for instance, is but two units; the number of four is reducible to one repeated four times. Therefore we cannot conceive any number without conceiving unity, which is the essential foundation of any possible number; nor can we conceive any repetition of units without conceiving unity itself, which is its basis.

But which way can I know any real unit? I never saw, nor so much as imagined any by the report of my senses. Let me take, for instance, the most subtle atom; it must have a figure, length, breadth, and depth, a top and a bottom, a left and a right side; and again the top is not the bottom, nor one side the other. Therefore this atom is not truly one, for it consists of parts. Now a compound is a real number, and a multitude of beings. It is not a real unit, but a collection of beings, one of which is not the other. I therefore never learnt by my eyes, my ears, my hands, nor even by my imagination, that there is in nature any real unity; on the contrary, neither my senses nor my imagination ever presented to me anything but what is a compound, a real number or a multitude. All unity continually escapes me; it flies me as it were by a kind of enchantment. Since I look for it in so many divisions of an atom, I certainly have a distinct idea of it; and it is only by its simple and clear idea that I arrive, by the repetition of it, at the knowledge of so many other numbers. But since it escapes me in all the divisions of the bodies of nature, it clearly follows that I never came by the knowledge of it, through the canal of my senses and imagination. Here therefore is an idea which is in me independently from the senses, imagination, and impressions of bodies.

Moreover, although I would not frankly acknowledge that I have a clear idea of unity, which is the foundation of all numbers, because they are but repetitions or collections of units: I must at least be forced to own that I know a great many numbers with their proprieties and relations. I know, for instance, how much make 900,000,000 joined with 800,000,000 of another sum. I make no mistake in it; and I should, with certainty, immediately rectify any man that should. Nevertheless, neither my senses nor my imagination were ever able to represent to me distinctly all those millions put together. Nor would the image they should represent to me be more like seventeen hundred millions than a far inferior number. Therefore, how came I by so distinct an idea of numbers, which I never could either feel or imagine? These ideas, independent upon bodies, can neither be corporeal nor admitted in a corporeal subject. They discover to me the nature of my soul, which admits what is incorporeal and receives it within itself in an incorporeal manner. Now, how came I by so incorporeal an idea of bodies themselves? I cannot by my own nature carry it within me, since what in me knows bodies is incorporeal; and since it knows them, without receiving that knowledge through the canal of corporeal organs, such as the senses and imagination. What thinks in me must be, as it were, a nothing of corporeal nature. How was I able to know beings that have by nature no relation with my thinking being? Certainly a being superior to those two natures, so very different, and which comprehends them both in its infinity, must have joined them in my soul, and given me an idea of a nature entirely different from that which thinks in me.

SECT. LXII. The Idea of the Unity proves that there are Immaterial Substances; and that there is a Being Perfectly One, who is God.

As for units, some perhaps will say that I do not know them by the bodies, but only by the spirits; and, therefore, that my mind being one, and truly known to me, it is by it, and not by the bodies, I have the idea of unity. But to this I answer.

It will, at least, follow from thence that I know substances that have no manner of extension or divisibility, and which are present. Here are already beings purely incorporeal, in the number of which I ought to place my soul. Now, who is it that has united it to my body? This soul of mine is not an infinite being; it has not been always, and it thinks within certain bounds. Now, again, who makes it know bodies so different from it? Who gives it so great a command over a certain body; and who gives reciprocally to that body so great a command over the soul? Moreover, which way do I know whether this thinking soul is really one, or whether it has parts? I do not see this soul. Now, will anybody say that it is in so invisible, and so impenetrable, a thing that I clearly see what unity is? I am so far from learning by my soul what the being One is, that, on the contrary, it is by the clear idea I have already of unity that I examine whether my soul be one or divisible.

Add to this, that I have within me a clear idea of a perfect unity, which is far above that I may find in my soul. The latter is often conscious that she is divided between two contrary opinions, inclinations, and habits. Now, does not this division, which I find within myself, show and denote a kind of multiplicity and composition of parts? Besides, the soul has, at least, a successive composition of thoughts, one of which is most different and distinct from another. I conceive an unity infinitely more One, if I may so speak. I conceive a Being who never changes His thoughts, who always thinks all things at once, and in which no composition, even successive, can be found. Undoubtedly it is the idea of the perfect and supreme unity that makes me so inquisitive after some unity in spirits, and even in bodies. This idea, ever present within me, is innate or inborn with me; it is the perfect model by which I seek everywhere some imperfect copy of the unity. This idea of what is one, simple, and indivisible by excellence can be no other than the idea of God. I, therefore, know God with such clearness and evidence, that it is by knowing Him I seek in all creatures, and in myself, some image and likeness of His unity. The bodies have, as it were, some mark or print of that unity, which still flies away in the division of its parts; and the spirits have a greater likeness of it, although they have a successive composition of thoughts.

SECT. LXIII. Dependence and Independence of Man. His Dependence Proves the Existence of his Creator.

But here is another mystery which I carry within me, and which makes me incomprehensible to my self, viz.: that on the one hand I am free, and on the other dependent. Let us examine these two things, and see whether it is possible to reconcile them.

I am a dependent being. Independency is the supreme perfection. To be by one's self is to carry within one's self the source or spring of one's own being; or, which is the same, it is to borrow nothing from any being different from one's self. Suppose a being that has all the perfections you can imagine, but which has a borrowed and dependent being, and you will find him to be less perfect than another being in which you would suppose but bare independency. For there is no comparison to be made between a being that exists by himself and a being who has nothing of his own—nothing but what is precarious and borrowed—and is in himself, as it were, only upon trust.

This consideration brings me to acknowledge the imperfection of what I call my soul. If she existed by herself, it would borrow nothing from another; she would not want either to be instructed in her ignorances, or to be rectified in her errors. Nothing could reclaim her from her vices, or inspire her with virtue; for nothing would be able to render her will better than it should have been at first. This soul would ever possess whatever she should be capable to enjoy, nor could she ever receive any addition from without. On the other hand, it is no less certain that she could not lose anything, for what is or exists by itself is always necessarily whatever it is. Therefore my soul could not fall into ignorance, error, or vice, or suffer any diminution of good-will; nor could she, on the other hand, instruct or correct herself, or become better than she is.

Now, I experience the contrary of all these; for I forget, mistake, err, go astray, lose the sight of truth and the love of virtue, I corrupt, I diminish. On the other hand, I improve and increase by acquiring wisdom and good-will, which I never had. This intimate experience convinces me that my soul is not a being existing by itself and independent; that is necessary, and immutable in all it possesses and enjoys. Now, whence proceeds this augmentation and improvement of myself? Who is it that can enlarge and perfect my being by making me better, and, consequently, greater than I was?

SECT. LXIV. Good Will cannot Proceed but from a Superior Being.

The will or faculty of willing is undoubtedly a degree of being, and of good, or perfection; but good-will, benevolence, or desire of good, is another degree of superior good. For one may misuse will in order to wish ill, cheat, hurt, or do injustice; whereas good-will is the good or right use of will itself, which cannot but be good. Good-will is therefore what is most precious in man. It is that which sets a value upon all the rest. It is, as it were, "The whole man:" Hoc enim omnis homo.

I have already shown that my will is not by itself, since it is liable to lose and receive degrees of good or perfection; and likewise that it is a good inferior to good-will, because it is better to will good than barely to have a will susceptible both of good and evil. How could I be brought to believe that I, a weak, imperfect, borrowed, precarious, and dependent being, bestow on myself the highest degree of perfection, while it is visible and evident that I derive the far inferior degree of perfection from a First Being? Can I imagine that God gives me the lesser good, and that I give myself the greater without Him? How should I come by that high degree of perfection in order to give it myself! Should I have it from nothing, which is all my own stock? Shall I say that other spirits, much like or equal to mine, give it me? But since those limited and dependent beings like myself cannot give themselves anything no more than I can, much less can they bestow anything upon another. For as they do not exist by themselves, so they have not by themselves any true power, either over me, or over things that are imperfect in me, or over themselves. Wherefore, without stopping with them, we must go up higher in order to find out a first, teeming, and most powerful cause, that is able to bestow on my soul the good will she has not.

SECT. LXV. As a Superior Being is the Cause of All the Modifications of Creatures, so it is Impossible for Man's Will to Will Good by Itself or of its own Accord.

Let us still add another reflection. That First Being is the cause of all the modifications of His creatures. The operation follows the Being, as the philosophers are used to speak. A being that is dependent in the essence of his being cannot but be dependent in all his operations, for the accessory follows the principal. Therefore, the Author of the essence of the being is also the Author of all the modifications or modes of being of creatures. Thus God is the real and immediate cause of all the configurations, combinations, and motions of all the bodies of the universe. It is by means or upon occasion of a body He has set in motion that He moves another. It is He who created everything and who does everything in His creatures or works. Now, volition is the modification of the will or willing faculty of the soul, just as motion is the modification of bodies. Shall we affirm that God is the real, immediate, and total cause of the motion of all bodies, and that He is not equally the real and immediate cause of the good-will of men's wills? Will this modification, the most excellent of all, be the only one not made by God in His own work, and which the work bestows on itself independently? Who can entertain such a thought? Therefore my good-will which I had not yesterday and which I have to-day is not a thing I bestow upon myself, but must come from Him who gave me both the will and the being.

As to will is a greater perfection than barely to be, so to will good is more perfect than to will. The step from power to a virtuous act is the greatest perfection in man. Power is only a balance or poise between virtue and vice, or a suspension between good and evil. The passage or step to the act is a decision or determination for the good, and consequent by the superior good. The power susceptible of good and evil comes from God, which we have fully evinced. Now, shall we affirm that the decisive stroke that determines to the greater good either is not at all, or is less owing to Him? All this evidently proves what the Apostle says, viz., that God "works both to will and to do of His good pleasure." Here is man's dependence; let us look for his liberty.

SECT. LXVI. Of Man's Liberty.

I am free, nor can I doubt of it. I am intimately and invincibly convinced that I can either will or not will, and that there is in me a choice not only between willing and not willing, but also between divers wills about the variety of objects that present themselves. I am sensible, as the Scripture says, that I "am in the hands of my Council," which alone suffices to show me that my soul is not corporeal. All that is body or corporeal does not in the least determine itself, and is, on the contrary, determined in all things by laws called physical, which are necessary, invincible, and contrary to what I call liberty. From thence I infer that my soul is of a nature entirely different from that of my body. Now who is it that was able to join by a reciprocal union two such different natures, and hold them in so just a concert for all their respective operations? That tie, as we observed before, cannot be formed but by a Superior Being, who comprehends and unites those two sorts of perfections in His own infinite perfection.

SECT. LXVII. Man's Liberty Consists in that his Will by determining, Modifies Itself.

It is not the same with the modification of my soul which is called will, and by some philosophers volition, as with the modifications of bodies. A body does not in the least modify itself, but is modified by the sole power of God. It does not move itself, it is moved; it does not act in anything, it is only acted and actuated. Thus God is the only real and immediate cause of all the different modifications of bodies. As for spirits the case is different, for my will determines itself. Now to determine one's self to a will is to modify one's self, and therefore my will modifies itself. God may prevent my soul, but He does not give it the will in the same manner as He gives motion to bodies. If it is God who modifies me, I modify myself with Him, and am with Him a real cause of my own will. My will is so much my own that I am only to blame if I do not will what I ought. When I will a thing it is in my power not to will it, and when I do not will it it is likewise in my power to will it. I neither am nor can be compelled in my will; for I cannot will what I actually will in spite of myself, since the will I mean evidently excludes all manner of constraint. Besides the exemption from all compulsion, I am likewise free from necessity.

I am conscious and sensible that I have, as it were, a two-edged will, which at its own choice may be either for the affirmative or the negative, the yes or the no, and turn itself either towards an object or towards another. I know no other reason or determination of my will but my will itself. I will a thing because I am free to will it; and nothing is so much in my power as either to will or not to will it. Although my will should not be constrained, yet if it were necessitated it would be as strongly and invincibly determined to will as bodies are to move. An invincible necessity would have as much influence over the will with respect to spirits as it has over motion with respect to bodies; and, in such a case, the will would be no more accountable for willing than a body for moving. It is true the will would will what it would; but the motion by which a body is moved is the same as the volition by which the willing faculty wills. If therefore volition be necessitated as motion it deserves neither more nor less praise or blame. For though a necessitated will may seem to be a will unconstrained, yet it is such a will as one cannot forbear having, and for which he that has it is not accountable. Nor does previous knowledge establish true liberty, for a will may be preceded by the knowledge of divers objects, and yet have no real election or choice. Nor is deliberation or the being in suspense any more than a vain trifle, if I deliberate between two counsels when I am under an actual impotency to follow the one and under an actual necessity to pursue the other. In short, there is no serious and true choice between two objects, unless they be both actually ready within my reach so that I may either leave or take which of the two I please.

SECT. LXVIII. Will may Resist Grace, and Its Liberty is the Foundation of Merit and Demerit.

When therefore I say I am free, I mean that my will is fully in my power, and that even God Himself leaves me at liberty to turn it which way I please, that I am not determined as other beings, and that I determine myself. I conceive that if that First Being prevents me, to inspire me with a good-will, it is still in my power to reject His actual inspiration, how strong soever it may be, to frustrate its effect, and to refuse my assent to it. I conceive likewise that when I reject His inspiration for the good, I have the true and actual power not to reject it; just as I have the actual and immediate power to rise when I remain sitting, and to shut my eyes when I have them open. Objects may indeed solicit me by all their allurements and agreeableness to will or desire them. The reasons for willing may present themselves to me with all their most lively and affecting attendants, and the Supreme Being may also attract me by His most persuasive inspirations. But yet for all this actual attraction of objects, cogency of reasons, and even inspiration of a Superior Being, I still remain master of my will, and am free either to will or not to will.

It is this exemption not only from all manner of constraint or compulsion but also from all necessity and this command over my own actions that render me inexcusable when I will evil, and praiseworthy when I will good; in this lies merit and demerit, praise and blame; it is this that makes either punishment or reward just; it is upon this consideration that men exhort, rebuke, threaten, and promise. This is the foundation of all policy, instruction, and rules of morality. The upshot of the merit and demerit of human actions rests upon this basis, that nothing is so much in the power of our will as our will itself, and that we have this free-will—this, as it were, two-edged faculty—and this elative power between two counsels which are immediately, as it were, within our reach. It is what shepherds and husbandmen sing in the fields, what merchants and artificers suppose in their traffic, what actors represent in public shows, what magistrates believe in their councils, what doctors teach in their schools; it is that, in short, which no man of sense can seriously call in question. That truth imprinted in the bottom of our hearts, is supposed in the practice, even by those philosophers who would endeavour to shake it by their empty speculations. The intimate evidence of that truth is like that of the first principles, which want no proof, and which serve themselves as proofs to other truths that are not so clear and self-evident. But how could the First Being make a creature who is himself the umpire of his own actions?

SECT. LXIX. A Character of the Deity, both in the Dependence and Independence of Man.

Let us now put together these two truths equally certain. I am dependent upon a First Being even in my own will; and nevertheless I am free. What then is this dependent liberty? how is it possible for a man to conceive a free-will, that is given by a First Being? I am free in my will, as God is in His. It is principally in this I am His image and likeness. What a greatness that borders upon infinite is here! This is a ray of the Deity itself: it is a kind of Divine power I have over my will; but I am but a bare image of that supreme Being so absolutely free and powerful.

The image of the Divine independence is not the reality of what it represents; and, therefore, my liberty is but a shadow of that First Being, by whom I exist and act. On the one hand, the power I have of willing evil is, indeed, rather a weakness and frailty of my will than a true power: for it is only a power to fall, to degrade myself, and to diminish my degree of perfection and being. On the other hand, the power I have to will good is not an absolute power, since I have it not of myself. Now liberty being no more than that power, a precarious and borrowed power can constitute but a precarious, borrowed, and dependent liberty; and, therefore, so imperfect and so precarious a being cannot but be dependent. But how is he free? What profound mystery is here! His liberty, of which I cannot doubt, shows his perfection; and his dependence argues the nothingness from which he was drawn.

SECT. LXX. The Seal and Stamp of the Deity in His Works.

We have seen the prints of the Deity, or to speak more properly, the seal and stamp of God Himself, in all that is called the works of nature. When a man will not enter into philosophical subtleties, he observes with the first cast of the eye a hand, that was the first mover, in all the parts of the universe, and set all the wheels of the great machine a-going. The heavens, the earth, the stars, plants, animals, our bodies, our minds: everything shows and proclaims an order, an exact measure, an art, a wisdom, a mind superior to us, which is, as it were, the soul of the whole world, and which leads and directs everything to his ends, with a gentle and insensible, though omnipotent, force. We have seen, as it were, the architecture and frame of the universe; the just proportion of all its parts; and the bare cast of the eye has sufficed us to find and discover even in an ant, more than in the sun, a wisdom and power that delights to exert itself in the polishing and adorning its vilest works. This is obvious, without any speculative discussion, to the most ignorant of men; but what a world of other wonders should we discover, should we penetrate into the secrets of physics, and dissect the inward parts of animals, which are framed according to the most perfect mechanics.

SECT. LXXI. Objection of the Epicureans, who Ascribe Everything to Chance, considered.

I hear certain philosophers who answer me that all this discourse on the art that shines in the universe is but a continued sophism. "All nature," will they say, "is for man's use, it is true; but you have no reason to infer from thence, that it was made with art, and on purpose for the use of man. A man must be ingenious in deceiving himself who looks for and thinks to find what never existed." "It is true," will they add, "that man's industry makes use of an infinite number of things that nature affords, and are convenient for him; but nature did not make those things on purpose for his conveniency. As, for instance, some country fellows climb up daily, by certain craggy and pointed rocks, to the top of a mountain; but yet it does not follow that those points of rocks were cut with art, like a staircase, for the conveniency of men. In like manner, when a man happens to be in the fields, during a stormy rain, and fortunately meets with a cave, he uses it, as he would do a house, for shelter; but, however, it cannot be affirmed that this cave was made on purpose to serve men for a house. It is the same with the whole world: it was formed by chance, and without design; but men finding it as it is, had the art to turn and improve it to their own uses. Thus the art you admire both in the work and its artificer, is only in men, who know how to make use of everything that surrounds them." This is certainly the strongest objection those philosophers can raise; and I hope they will have no reason to complain that I have weakened it; but it will immediately appear how weak it is in itself when closely examined. The bare repetition of what I said before will be sufficient to demonstrate it.

SECT. LXXII. Answer to the Objection of the Epicureans, who Ascribe all to Chance.

What would one say of a man who should set up for a subtle philosopher, or, to use the modern expression, a free-thinker, and who entering a house should maintain it was made by chance, and that art had not in the least contributed to render it commodious to men, because there are caves somewhat like that house, which yet were never dug by the art of man? One should show to such a reasoner all the parts of the house, and tell him for instance:—Do you see this great court-gate? It is larger than any door, that coaches may enter it. This court has sufficient space for coaches to turn in it. This staircase is made up of low steps, that one may ascend it with ease; and turns according to the apartments and stories it is to serve. The windows, opened at certain distances, light the whole building. They are glazed, lest the wind should enter with the light; but they may be opened at pleasure, in order to breathe a sweet air when the weather is fair. The roof is contrived to defend the whole house from the injuries of the air. The timber-work is laid slanting and pointed at the top, that the rain and snow may easily slide down on both sides. The tiles bear one upon another, that they may cover the timber-work. The divers floors serve to make different stories, in order to multiply lodgings within a small space. The chimneys are contrived to light fire in winter without setting the house on fire, and to let out the smoke, lest it should offend those that warm themselves. The apartments are distributed in such a manner that they be disengaged from one another; that a numerous family may lodge in the house, and the one not be obliged to pass through another's room; and that the master's apartment be the principal. There are kitchens, offices, stables, and coach-houses. The rooms are furnished with beds to lie in, chairs to sit on, and tables to write and eat on. Sure, should one urge to that philosopher, this work must have been directed by some skilful architect; for everything in it is agreeable, pleasant, proportioned, and commodious; and besides, he must needs have had excellent artists under him. "Not at all," would such a philosopher answer; "you are ingenious in deceiving yourself. It is true this house is pleasant, agreeable, proportioned, and commodious; but yet it made itself with all its proportions. Chance put together all the stones in this excellent order; it raised the walls, jointed and laid the timber-work, cut open the casements, and placed the staircase: do not believe any human hand had anything to do with it. Men only made the best of this piece of work when they found it ready made. They fancy it was made for them, because they observe things in it which they know how to improve to their own conveniency; but all they ascribe to the design and contrivance of an imaginary architect, is but the effect of their preposterous imaginations. This so regular, and so well-contrived house, was made in just the same manner as a cave, and men finding it ready made to their hands made use of it, as they would in a storm, of a cave they should find under a rock in a desert."

What thoughts could a man entertain of such a fantastic philosopher, if he should persist seriously to assert that such a house displays no art? When we read the fabulous story of Amphion, who by a miraculous effect of harmony caused the stones to rise, and placed themselves, with order and symmetry, one on the top of another, in order to form the walls of Thebes, we laugh and sport with that poetical fiction: but yet this very fiction is not so incredible as that which the free-thinking philosopher we contend with would dare to maintain. We might, at least, imagine that harmony, which consists in a local motion of certain bodies, might (by some of those secret virtues, which we admire in nature, without being acquainted with them) shake and move the stones into a certain order and in a sort of cadence, which might occasion some regularity in the building. I own this explanation both shocks and clashes with reason; but yet it is less extravagant than what I have supposed a philosopher should say. What, indeed, can be more absurd, than to imagine stones that hew themselves, that go out of the quarry, that get one on the top of another, without leaving any empty space; that carry with them mortar to cement one another; that place themselves in different ranks for the contrivance of apartments; and who admit on the top of all the timber-roof, with the tiles, in order to cover the whole work? The very children, that cannot yet speak plain, would laugh, if they were seriously told such a ridiculous story.

SECT. LXXIII. Comparison of the World with a Regular House. A Continuation of the Answer to the Objection of the Epicureans.

But why should it appear less ridiculous to hear one say that the world made itself, as well as that fabulous house? The question is not to compare the world with a cave without form, which is supposed to be made by chance: but to compare it with a house in which the most perfect architecture should be conspicuous. For the structure and frame of the least living creature is infinitely more artful and admirable than the finest house that ever was built.

Suppose a traveller entering Saida, the country where the ancient Thebes, with a hundred gates, stood formerly, and which is now a desert, should find there columns, pyramids, obelisks, and inscriptions in unknown characters. Would he presently say: men never inhabited this place; no human hand had anything to do here; it is chance that formed these columns, that placed them on their pedestals, and crowned them with their capitals, with such just proportions; it is chance that so firmly jointed the pieces that make up these pyramids; it is chance that cut the obelisks in one single stone, and engraved in them these characters? Would he not, on the contrary, say, with all the certainty the mind of man is capable of: these magnificent ruins are the remains of a noble and majestical architecture that flourished in ancient Egypt? This is what plain reason suggests, at the first cast of the eye, or first sight, and without reasoning. It is the same with the bare prospect of the universe. A man may by vain, long-winded, preposterous reasonings confound his own reason and obscure the clearest notions: but the single cast of the eye is decisive. Such a work as the world is never makes itself of its own accord. There is more art and proportion in the bones, tendons, veins, arteries, nerves, and muscles, that compose man's body, than in all the architecture of the ancient Greeks and Egyptians. The single eye of the least of living creatures surpasses the mechanics of all the most skilful artificers. If a man should find a watch in the sands of Africa, he would never have the assurance seriously to affirm, that chance formed it in that wild place; and yet some men do not blush to say that the bodies of animals, to the artful framing of which no watch can ever be compared, are the effects of the caprices of chance.

SECT. LXXIV. Another Objection of the Epicureans drawn from the Eternal Motion of Atoms.

I am not ignorant of a reasoning which the Epicureans may frame into an objection. "The atoms will, they say, have an eternal motion; their fortuitous concourse must, in that eternity, have already produced infinite combinations. Who says infinite, says what comprehends all without exception. Amongst these infinite combinations of atoms which have already happened successively, all such as are possible must necessarily be found: for if there were but one possible combination, beyond those contained in that infinite, it would cease to be a true infinite, because something might be added to it; and whatever may be increased, being limited on the side it may receive an addition, is not truly infinite. Hence it follows that the combination of atoms, which makes up the present system of the world, is one of the combinations which the atoms have had successively: which being laid as a principle, is it matter of wonder that the world is as it is now? It must have taken this exact form, somewhat sooner, or somewhat later, for in some one of these infinite changes it must, at last, have received that combination that makes it now appear so regular; since it must have had, by turns, all combinations that can be conceived. All systems are comprehended in the total of eternity. There is none but the concourse of atoms, forms, and embraces, sooner or later. In that infinite variety of new spectacles of nature, the present was formed in its turn. We find ourselves actually in this system. The concourse of atoms that made will, in process of time, unmake it, in order to make others, ad infinitum, of all possible sorts. This system could not fail having its place, since all others without exception are to have theirs, each in its turn. It is in vain one looks for a chimerical art in a work which chance must have made as it is.

"An example will suffice to illustrate this. I suppose an infinite number of combinations of the letters of the alphabet, successively formed by chance. All possible combinations are, undoubtedly, comprehended in that total, which is truly infinite. Now, it is certain that Homer's Iliad is but a combination of letters: therefore Homer's Iliad is comprehended in that infinite collection of combinations of the characters of the alphabet. This being laid down as a principle, a man who will assign art in the Iliad, will argue wrong. He may extol the harmony of the verses, the justness and magnificence of the expressions, the simplicity and liveliness of images, the due proportion of the parts of the poem, its perfect unity, and inimitable conduct; he may object that chance can never make anything so perfect, and that the utmost effort of human wit is hardly capable to finish so excellent a piece of work: yet all in vain, for all this specious reasoning is visibly false. It is certain, on the contrary, that the fortuitous concourse of characters, putting them together by turns with an infinite variety, the precise combination that composes the Iliad must have happened in its turn, somewhat sooner or somewhat later. It has happened at last; and thus the Iliad is perfect, without the help of any human art." This is the objection fairly laid down in its full latitude; I desire the reader's serious and continued attention to the answers I am going to make to it.

SECT. LXXV. Answers to the Objection of the Epicureans drawn from the Eternal Motion of Atoms.

Nothing can be more absurd than to speak of successive combinations of atoms infinite in number; for the infinite can never be either successive or divisible. Give me, for instance, any number you may pretend to be infinite, and it will still be in my power to do two things that shall demonstrate it not to be a true infinite. In the first place, I can take an unit from it; and in such a case it will become less than it was, and will certainly be finite; for whatever is less than the infinite has a boundary or limit on the side where one stops, and beyond which one might go. Now the number which is finite as soon as one takes from it one single unit, could not be infinite before that diminution; for an unit is certainly finite, and a finite joined with another finite cannot make an infinite. If a single unit added to a finite number made an infinite, it would follow from thence that the finite would be almost equal to the infinite; than which nothing can be more absurd. In the second place, I may add an unit to that number given, and consequently increase it. Now what may be increased is not infinite, for the infinite can have no bound; and what is capable of augmentation is bounded on the side a man stops, when he might go further and add some units to it. It is plain, therefore, that no divisible compound can be the true infinite.

This foundation being laid, all the romance of the Epicurean philosophy disappears and vanishes out of sight in an instant. There never can be any divisible body truly infinite in extent, nor any number or any succession that is a true infinite. From hence it follows that there never can be an infinite successive number of combinations of atoms. If this chimerical infinite were real, I own all possible and conceivable combinations of atoms would be found in it; and that consequently all combinations that seem to require the utmost industry would likewise be included in them. In such a case, one might ascribe to mere chance the most marvellous performances of art. If one should see palaces built according to the most perfect rules of architecture, curious furniture, watches, clocks, and all sort of machines the most compounded, in a desert island, he should not be free reasonably to conclude that there have been men in that island who made all those exquisite works. On the contrary, he ought to say, "Perhaps one of the infinite combinations of atoms which chance has successively made, has formed all these compositions in this desert island without the help of any man's art;" for such an assertion is a natural consequence of the principles of the Epicureans. But the very absurdity of the consequence serves to expose the extravagance of the principle they lay down. When men, by the natural rectitude of their common sense, conclude that such sort of works cannot result from chance, they visibly suppose, though in a confused manner, that atoms are not eternal, and that in their fortuitous concourse they had not an infinite succession of combinations. For if that principle were admitted, it would no longer be possible ever to distinguish the works of art from those that should result from those combinations as fortuitous as a throw at dice.

SECT. LXXVI. The Epicureans confound the Works of Art with those of Nature.

All men who naturally suppose a sensible difference between the works of art and those of chance do consequently, though but implicitly, suppose that the combinations of atoms were not infinite—which supposition is very just. This infinite succession of combinations of atoms is, as I showed before, a more absurd chimera than all the absurdities some men would explain by that false principle. No number, either successive or continual, can be infinite; from whence it follows that the number of atoms cannot be infinite, that the succession of their various motions and combinations cannot be infinite, that the world cannot be eternal, and that we must find out a precise and fixed beginning of these successive combinations. We must recur to a first individual in the generations of every species. We must likewise find out the original and primitive form of every particle of matter that makes a part of the universe. And as the successive changes of that matter must be limited in number, we must not admit in those different combinations but such as chance commonly produces; unless we acknowledge a Superior Being, who with the perfection of art made the wonderful works which chance could never have made.

SECT. LXXVII. The Epicureans take whatever they please for granted, without any Proof.

The Epicurean philosophers are so weak in their system that it is not in their power to form it, or bring it to bear, unless one admits without proofs their most fabulous postulata and positions. In the first place they suppose eternal atoms, which is begging the question; for how can they make out that atoms have ever existed and exist by themselves? To exist by one's self is the supreme perfection. Now, what authority have they to suppose, without proofs, that atoms have in themselves a perfect, eternal, and immutable being? Do they find this perfection in the idea they have of every atom in particular? An atom not being the same with, and being absolutely distinguished from, another atom, each of them must have in itself eternity and independence with respect to any other being. Once more, is it in the idea these philosophers have of each atom that they find this perfection? But let us grant them all they suppose in this question, and even what they ought to be ashamed to suppose—viz., that atoms are eternal, subsisting by themselves, independent from any other being, and consequently entirely perfect.

SECT. LXXVIII. The Suppositions of the Epicureans are False and Chimerical.

Must we suppose, besides, that atoms have motion of themselves? Shall we suppose it out of gaiety to give an air of reality to a system more chimerical than the tales of the fairies? Let us consult the idea we have of a body. We conceive it perfectly well without supposing it to be in motion, and represent it to us at rest; nor is its idea in this state less clear; nor does it lose its parts, figure, or dimensions. It is to no purpose to suppose that all bodies are perpetually in some motion, either sensible or insensible; and that though some parts of matter have a lesser motion than others, yet the universal mass of matter has ever the same motion in its totality. To speak at this rate is building castles in the air, and imposing vain imaginations on the belief of others; for who has told these philosophers that the mass of matter has ever the same motion in its totality? Who has made the experiment of it? Have they the assurance to bestow the name of philosophy upon a rash fiction which takes for granted what they never can make out? Is there no more to do than to suppose whatever one pleases in order to elude the most simple and most constant truths? What authority have they to suppose that all bodies incessantly move, either sensibly or insensibly? When I see a stone that appears motionless, how will they prove to me that there is no atom in that stone but what is actually in motion? Will they ever impose upon me bare suppositions, without any semblance of truth, for decisive proofs?

SECT. LXXIX. It is Falsely supposed that Motion is Essential to Bodies.

However, let us go a step further, and, out of excessive complaisance, suppose that all the bodies in Nature are actually in motion. Does it follow from thence that motion is essential to every particle of matter? Besides, if all bodies have not an equal degree of motion; if some move sensibly, and more swiftly than others; if the same body may move sometimes quicker and sometimes slower; if a body that moves communicates its motion to the neighbouring body that was at rest, or in such inferior motion that it was insensible—it must be confessed that a mode or modification which sometimes increases, and at other times decreases, in bodies is not essential to them. What is essential to a being is ever the same in it. Neither the motion that varies in bodies, and which, after having increased, slackens and decreases to such a degree as to appear absolutely extinct and annihilated; nor the motion that is lost, that is communicated, that passes from one body to another as a foreign thing—can belong to the essence of bodies. And, therefore, I may conclude that bodies are perfect in their essence without ascribing to them any motion. If they have no motion in their essence, they have it only by accident; and if they have it only by accident, we must trace up that accident to its true cause. Bodies must either bestow motion on themselves, or receive it from some other being. It is evident they do not bestow it on themselves, for no being can give what it has not in itself. And we are sensible that a body at rest ever remains motionless, unless some neighbouring body happens to shake it. It is certain, therefore, that no body moves by itself, and is only moved by some other body that communicates its motion to it. But how comes it to pass that a body can move another? What is the reason that a ball which a man causes to roll on a smooth table (billiards, for the purpose) cannot touch another without moving it? Why was it not possible that motion should not ever communicate itself from one body to another? In such a case a ball in motion would stop near another at their meeting, and yet never shake it.

SECT. LXXX. The Rules of Motion, which the Epicureans suppose do not render it essential to Bodies.

I may be answered that, according to the rules of motion among bodies, one ought to shake or move another. But where are those laws of motion written and recorded? Who both made them and rendered them so inviolable? They do not belong to the essence of bodies, for we can conceive bodies at rest; and we even conceive bodies that would not communicate their motion to others unless these rules, with whose original we are unacquainted, subjected them to it. Whence comes this, as it were, arbitrary government of motion over all bodies? Whence proceed laws so ingenious, so just, so well adapted one to the other, that the least alteration of or deviation from which would, on a sudden, overturn and destroy all the excellent order we admire in the universe? A body being entirely distinct from another, is in its nature absolutely independent from it in all respects. Whence it follows that it should not receive anything from it, or be susceptible of any of its impressions. The modifications of a body imply no necessary reason to modify in the same manner another body, whose being is entirely independent from the being of the first. It is to no purpose to allege that the most solid and most heavy bodies carry or force away those that are less big and less solid; and that, according to this rule, a great leaden ball ought to move a great ball of ivory. We do not speak of the fact; we only inquire into the cause of it. The fact is certain, and therefore the cause ought likewise to be certain and precise. Let us look for it without any manner of prepossession or prejudice. What is the reason that a great body carries off a little one? The thing might as naturally happen quite otherwise; for it might as well happen that the most solid body should never move any other body—that is to say, motion might be incommunicable. Nothing but custom obliges us to suppose that Nature ought to act as it does.

SECT. LXXXI. To give a satisfactory Account of Motion we must recur to the First Mover.

Moreover, it has been proved that matter cannot be either infinite or eternal; and, therefore, there must be supposed both a first atom (by which motion must have begun at a precise moment), and a first concourse of atoms (that must have formed the first combination). Now, I ask what mover gave motion to that first atom, and first set the great machine of the universe a-going? It is not possible to elude this home question by an endless circle, for this question, lying within a finite circumference, must have an end at last; and so we must find the first atom in motion, and the first moment of that first motion, together with the first mover, whose hand made that first impression.

SECT. LXXXII. No Law of Motion has its Foundation in the Essence of the Body; and most of those Laws are Arbitrary.

Among the laws of motion we must look upon all those as arbitrary which we cannot account for by the very essence of bodies. We have already made out that no motion is essential to any body. Wherefore all those laws which are supposed to be eternal and immutable are, on the contrary, arbitrary, accidental, and made without cogent necessity; for there is none of them that can be accounted for by the essence of bodies.

If there were any law of motion essential to bodies, it would undoubtedly be that by which bodies of less bulk and less solid are moved by such as have more bulk and solidity. And yet we have seen that that very law is not to be accounted for by the essence of bodies. There is another which might also seem very natural— that, I mean, by which bodies ever move rather in a direct than a crooked line, unless their motion be otherwise determined by the meeting of other bodies. But even this rule has no foundation in the essence of matter. Motion is so very accidental, and super-added to the nature of bodies, that we do not find in this nature of bodies any primitive or immutable law by which they ought to move at all, much less to move according to certain rules. In the same manner as bodies might have existed, and yet have never either been in motion or communicated motion one to another, so they might never have moved but in a circular line, and this motion might have been as natural to them as the motion in a direct line. Now, who is it that pitched upon either of these two laws equally possible? What is not determined by the essence of bodies can have been determined by no other but Him who gave bodies the motion they had not in their own essence. Besides, this motion in a direct line might have been upwards or downwards, from right to left, or from left to right, or in a diagonal line. Now, who is it that determined which way the straight line should go?

SECT. LXXXIII. The Epicureans can draw no Consequence from all their Suppositions, although the same should be granted them.

Let us still attend the Epicureans even in their most fabulous suppositions, and carry on the fiction to the last degree of complaisance. Let us admit motion in the essence of bodies, and suppose, as they do, that motion in a direct line is also essential to all atoms. Let us bestow upon atoms both a will and an understanding, as poets did on rocks and rivers. And let us allow them likewise to choose which way they will begin their straight line. Now, what advantage will these philosophers draw from all I have granted them, contrary to all evidence? In the first place, all atoms must have been in motion from all eternity; secondly, they must all have had an equal motion; thirdly, they must all have moved in a direct line; fourthly, they must all have moved by an immutable and essential law.

I am still willing to gratify our adversaries, so far as to suppose that those atoms are of different figures, for I will allow them to take for granted what they should be obliged to prove, and for which they have not so much as the shadow of a proof. One can never grant too much to men who never can draw any consequence from what is granted them; for the more absurdities are allowed them, the sooner they are caught by their own principles.

SECT. LXXXIV. Atoms cannot make any Compound by the Motion the Epicureans assign them.

These atoms of so many odd figures—some round, some crooked, others triangular, &c.—are by their essence obliged always to move in a straight line, without ever deviating or bending to the right or to the left; wherefore they never can hook one another, or make together any compound. Put, if you please, the sharpest hooks near other hooks of the like make; yet if every one of them never moves otherwise than in a line perfectly straight, they will eternally move one near another, in parallel lines, without being able to join and hook one another. The two straight lines which are supposed to be parallel, though immediate neighbours, will never cross one another, though carried on ad infinitum; wherefore in all eternity, no hooking, and consequently no compound, can result from that motion of atoms in a direct line.

SECT. LXXXV. The Clinamen, Declination, or Sending of Atoms is a Chimerical Notion that throws the Epicureans into a gross Contradiction.

The Epicureans, not being able to shut their eyes against this glaring difficulty, that strikes at the very foundation of their whole system, have, for a last shift, invented what Lucretius calls clinamen—by which is meant a motion somewhat declining or bending from the straight line, and which gives atoms the occasion to meet and encounter. Thus they turn and wind them at pleasure, according as they fancy best for their purpose. But upon what authority do they suppose this declination of atoms, which comes so pat to bear up their system? If motion in a straight line be essential to bodies, nothing can bend, nor consequently join them, in all eternity; the clinamen destroys the very essence of matter, and those philosophers contradict themselves without blushing. If, on the contrary, the motion in a direct line is not essential to all bodies, why do they so confidently suppose eternal, necessary, and immutable laws for the motion of atoms without recurring to a first mover? And why do they build a whole system of philosophy upon the precarious foundation of a ridiculous fiction? Without the clinamen the straight line can never produce anything, and the Epicurean system falls to the ground; with the clinamen, a fabulous poetical invention, the direct line is violated, and the system falls into derision and ridicule.

Both the straight line and the clinamen are airy suppositions and mere dreams; but these two dreams destroy each other, and this is the upshot of the uncurbed licentiousness some men allow themselves of supposing as eternal truths whatever their imagination suggests them to support a fable; while they refuse to acknowledge the artful and powerful hand that formed and placed all the parts of the universe.

SECT. LXXXVI. Strange Absurdity of the Epicureans, who endeavour to account for the Nature of the Soul by the Declination of Atoms.

To reach the highest degree of amazing extravagance, the Epicureans have had the assurance to explain and account for what we call the soul of man and his free-will, by the clinamen, which is so unaccountable and inexplicable itself. Thus they are reduced to affirm that it is in this motion, wherein atoms are in a kind of equilibrium between a straight line and a line somewhat circular, that human will consists.

Strange philosophy! If atoms move only in a straight line, they are inanimate, and incapable of any degree of knowledge, understanding, or will; but if the very same atoms somewhat deviate from the straight line, they become, on a sudden, animate, thinking, and rational. They are themselves intelligent souls, that know themselves, reflect, deliberate, and are free in their acts and determinations. Was there ever a more absurd metamorphosis?

What opinion would men have of religion if, in order to assert it, one should lay down principles and positions so trifling and ridiculous as theirs who dare to attack it in earnest?

SECT. LXXXVII. The Epicureans cast a Mist before their own Eyes by endeavouring to explain the Liberty of Man by the Declination of Atoms.

But let us consider to what degree those philosophers impose upon their own understandings. What can they find in the clinamen that, with any colour, can account for the liberty of man? This liberty is not imaginary; for it is not in our power to doubt of our free-will, any more than it is to doubt of what we are intimately conscious and certain. I am conscious I am free to continue sitting when I rise in order to walk. I am sensible of it with so entire certainty that it is not in my power ever to doubt of it in earnest; and I should be inconsistent with myself if I dared to say the contrary. Can the proof of our religion be more evident and convincing? We cannot doubt of the existence of God unless we doubt of our own liberty; from whence I infer that no man can seriously doubt of the being of the Deity, since no man can entertain a serious doubt about his own liberty. If, on the contrary, it be frankly acknowledged that men are really free, nothing is more easy than to demonstrate that the liberty of man's will cannot consist of any combination of atoms, if one supposes that there was no first mover, who gave matter arbitrary laws for its motion. Motion must be essential to bodies, and all the laws of motion must also be as necessary as the essences of natures are. Therefore, according to this system, all the motions of bodies must be performed by constant, necessary, and immutable laws; the motion in a straight line must be essential to all atoms, that are not made to deviate from it by the encounter of other atoms; the straight line must likewise be essential either upwards or downwards, either from right to left, or left to right, or some other diagonal way, fixed, precise, and immutable. Besides, it is evident that no atom can make another atom deviate; for that other atom carries also in its essence the same invincible and eternal determination to follow the straight line the same way. From hence it follows that all the atoms placed at first on different lines must pursue ad infinitum those parallel lines without ever coming nearer one another; and that those who are in the same line must follow one another ad infinitum without ever coming up together, but keeping still the same distance from one another. The clinamen, as we have already shown, is manifestly impossible: but, contrary to evident truth, supposing it to be possible, in such a case it must be affirmed that the clinamen is no less necessary, immutable, and essential to atoms than the straight line. Now, will anybody say that an essential and immutable law of the local motion of atoms explains and accounts for the true liberty of man? Is it not manifest that the clinamen can no more account for it than the straight line itself? The clinamen, supposing it to be true, would be as necessary as the perpendicular line, by which a stone falls from the top of a tower into the street. Is that stone free in its fall? However, the will of man, according to the principle of the clinamen, has no more freedom than that stone. Is it possible for man to be so extravagant as to dare to contradict his own conscience about his free-will, lest he should be forced to acknowledge his God and maker? To affirm, on the one hand, that the liberty of man is imaginary, we must silence the voice and stifle the sense of all nature; give ourselves the lie in the grossest manner; deny what we are most intimately conscious and certain of; and, in short, be reduced to believe that we have no eligibility or choice of two courses, or things proposed, about which we fairly deliberate upon any occasion. Nothing does religion more honour than to see men necessitated to fall into such gross and monstrous extravagance as soon as they call in question the truths she teaches. On the other hand, if we own that man is truly free, we acknowledge in him a principle that never can be seriously accounted for, either by the combinations of atoms or the laws of local motion, which must be supposed to be all equally necessary and essential to matter, if one denies a first mover. We must therefore go out of the whole compass of matter, and search far from combined atoms some incorporeal principle to account for free-will, if we admit it fairly. Whatever is matter and an atom, moves only by necessary, immutable, and invincible laws: wherefore liberty cannot be found either in bodies, or in any local motion; and so we must look for it in some incorporeal being. Now whose hand tied and subjected to the organs of this corporeal machine that incorporeal being which must necessarily be in me united to my body? Where is the artificer that ties and unites natures so vastly different? Can any but a power superior both to bodies and spirits keep them together in this union with so absolute a sway? Two crooked atoms, says an Epicurean, hook one another. Now this is false, according to his very system; for I have demonstrated that those two crooked atoms never hook one another, because they never meet. But, however, after having supposed that two crooked atoms unite by hooking one another, the Epicurean must be forced to own that the thinking being, which is free in his operations, and which consequently is not a collection of atoms, ever moved by necessary laws, is incorporeal, and could not by its figure be hooked with the body it animates. Thus which way so ever the Epicurean turns, he overthrows his system with his own hands. But let us not, by any means, endeavour to confound men that err and mistake, since we are men as well as they, and no less subject to error. Let us only pity them, study to light and inform them with patience, edify them, pray for them, and conclude with asserting an evident truth.

SECT. LXXXVIII. We must necessarily acknowledge the Hand of a First Cause in the Universe without inquiring why that first Cause has left Defects in it.

Thus everything in the universe—the heavens, the earth, plants, animals, and, above all, men—bears the stamp of a Deity. Everything shows and proclaims a set design, and a series and concatenation of subordinate causes, over-ruled and directed with order by a superior cause.

It is preposterous and foolish to criticise upon this great work. The defects that happen to be in it proceed either from the free and disorderly will of man, which produces them by its disorder, or from the ever holy and just will of God, who sometimes has a mind to punish impious men, and at other times by the wicked to exercise and improve the good. Nay, it happens oftentimes that what appears a defect to our narrow judgment in a place separate from the work is an ornament with respect to the general design, which we are not able to consider with views sufficiently extended and simple to know the perfection of the whole. Does not daily experience show that we rashly censure certain parts of men's works for want of being thoroughly acquainted with the whole extent of their designs and schemes? This happens, in particular, every day with respect to the works of painters and architects. If writing characters were of an immense bigness, each character at close view would take up a man's whole sight, so that it would not be possible for him to see above one at once; and, therefore, he would not be able to read—that is, put different letters together, and discover the sense of all those characters put together. It is the same with the great strokes of Providence in the conduct of the whole world during a long succession of ages. There is nothing but the whole that is intelligible; and the whole is too vast and immense to be seen at close view. Every event is like a particular character that is too large for our narrow organs, and which signifies nothing of itself and separate from the rest. When, at the consummation of ages, we shall see in God—that is, in the true point and centre of perspective—the total of human events, from the first to the last day of the universe, together with their proportions with regard to the designs of God, we shall cry out, "Lord, Thou alone art just and wise!" We cannot rightly judge of the works of men but by examining the whole. Every part ought not to have every perfection, but only such as becomes it according to the order and proportion of the different parts that compose the whole. In a human body, for instance, all the members must not be eyes, for there must be hands, feet, &c. So in the universe, there must be a sun for the day, but there must be also a moon for the night. Nec tibi occurrit perfecta universitas, nisi ubi majora sic præsto sunt, ut minora non desint. This is the judgment we ought to make of every part with respect to the whole. Any other view is narrow and deceitful. But what are the weak and puny designs of men, if compared to that of the creation and government of the universe? "As much as the heavens are above the earth, as much," says God in the Holy Writ, "are My ways and My thoughts above yours." Let, therefore, man admire what he understands, and be silent about what he does not comprehend. But, after all, even the real defects of this work are only imperfections which God was pleased to leave in it, to put us in mind that He drew and made it from nothing. There is not anything in the universe but what does and ought equally to bear these two opposite characters: on the one side, the seal or stamp of the artificer upon his work, and, on the other, the mark of its original nothing, into which it may relapse and dwindle every moment. It is an incomprehensible mixture of low and great; of frailty in the matter, and of art in the maker? The hand of God is conspicuous in everything, even in a worm that crawls on earth. Nothingness, on the other hand, appears everywhere, even in the most vast and most sublime genius. Whatever is not God, can have but a stinted perfection; and what has but a stinted perfection, always remains imperfect on the side where the boundary is sensible, and denotes that it might be improved. If the creature wanted nothing, it would be the Creator Himself; for it would have the fulness of perfection, which is the Deity itself. Since it cannot be infinite, it must be limited in perfection, that is, it must be imperfect on one side or other. It may have more or less imperfection, but still it must be imperfect. We must ever be able to point out the very place where it is defective, and to say, upon a critical examination, "This is what it might have had, what it has not."

SECT. LXXXIX. The Defects of the Universe compared with those of a Picture.

Do we conclude that a piece of painting is made by chance when we see in it either shades, or even some careless touches? The painter, we say, might have better finished those carnations, those draperies, those prospects. It is true, this picture is not perfect according to the nicest rules of art. But how extravagant would it be to say, "This picture is not absolutely perfect; therefore it is only a collection of colours formed by chance, nor did the hand of any painter meddle with it!" Now, what a man would blush to say of an indifferent and almost artless picture he is not ashamed to affirm of the universe, in which a crowd of incomprehensible wonders, with excellent order and proportion, are conspicuous. Let a man study the world as much as he pleases; let him descend into the minutest details; dissect the vilest of animals; narrowly consider the least grain of corn sown in the ground, and the manner in which it germinates and multiplies; attentively observe with what precautions a rose-bud blows and opens in the sun, and closes again at night; and he will find in all these more design, conduct, and industry than in all the works of art. Nay, what is called the art of men is but a faint imitation of the great art called the laws of Nature, and which the impious did not blush to call blind chance. Is it therefore a wonder that poets animated the whole universe, bestowed wings upon the winds, and arrows on the sun, and described great rivers impetuously running to precipitate themselves into the sea, and trees shooting up to heaven to repel the rays of the sun by their thick shades? These images and figures have also been received in the language of the vulgar, so natural it is for men to be sensible of the wonderful art that fills all nature. Poetry did only ascribe to inanimate creatures the art and design of the Creator, who does everything in them. From the figurative language of the poets those notions passed into the theology of the heathens, whose divines were the poets. They supposed an art, a power, or a wisdom, which they called numen, in creatures the most destitute of understanding. With them great rivers were gods; and springs, naiads. Woods and mountains had their particular deities; flowers had their Flora; and fruits, Pomona. After all, the more a man contemplates Nature, the more he discovers in it an inexhaustible stock of wisdom, which is, as it were, the soul of the universe.

SECT. XC. We must necessarily conclude that there is a First Being that created the Universe.

What must we infer from thence? The consequence flows of itself. "If so much wisdom and penetration," says Minutius Felix, "are required to observe the wonderful order and design of the structure of the world, how much more were necessary to form it!" If men so much admire philosophers, because they discover a small part of the wisdom that made all things, they must be stark blind not to admire that wisdom itself.

SECT. XCI. Reasons why Men do not acknowledge God in the Universe, wherein He shows Himself to them, as in a faithful glass.

This is the great object of the universe, wherein God, as it were in a glass, shows Himself to mankind. But some (I mean, the philosophers) were bewildered in their own thoughts. Everything with them turned into vanity. By their subtle reasonings some of them overshot and lost a truth which a man finds naturally and simply in himself without the help of philosophy.

Others, intoxicated by their passions, live in a perpetual avocation of thought. To perceive God in His works a man must, at least, consider them with attention. But passions cast such a mist before the eyes, not only of wild savages, but even of nations that seem to be most civilised and polite, that they do not so much as see the light that lights them. In this respect the Egyptians, Grecians, and Romans were no less blind or less brutish than the rudest and most ignorant Americans. Like these, they lay, as it were, buried within sensible things without going up higher; and they cultivated their wit, only to tickle themselves with softer sensations, without observing from what spring they proceeded. In this manner the generality of men pass away their lives upon earth. Say nothing to them, and they will think on nothing except what flatters either their brutish passions or vanity. Their souls grow so heavy and unwieldy that they cannot raise their thoughts to any incorporeal object. Whatever is not palpable and cannot be seen, tasted, heard, felt, or told, appears chimerical to them. This weakness of the soul, turning into unbelief, appears strength of mind to them; and their vanity glories in opposing what naturally strikes and affects the rest of mankind, just as if a monster prided in not being formed according to the common rules of Nature, or as if one born blind boasted of his unbelief with respect to light and colours, which other men perceive and discern.

SECT. XCII. A Prayer to God.

O my God, if so many men do not discover Thee in this great spectacle Thou givest them of all Nature, it is not because Thou art far from any of us. Every one of us feels Thee, as it were, with his hand; but the senses, and the passions they raise, take up all the attention of our minds. Thus, O Lord, Thy light shines in darkness; but darkness is so thick and gloomy that it does not admit the beams of Thy light. Thou appearest everywhere; and everywhere unattentive mortals neglect to perceive Thee. All Nature speaks of Thee and resounds with Thy holy name; but she speaks to deaf men, whose deafness proceeds from the noise and clutter they make to stun themselves. Thou art near and within them; but they are fugitive, and wandering, as it were, out of themselves. They would find Thee, O Sweet Light, O Eternal Beauty, ever old and ever young, O Fountain of Chaste Delights, O Pure and Happy Life of all who live truly, should they look for Thee within themselves. But the impious lose Thee only by losing themselves. Alas! Thy very gifts, which should show them the hand from whence they flow, amuse them to such a degree as to hinder them from perceiving it. They live by Thee, and yet they live without thinking on Thee; or, rather, they die by the Fountain of Life for want of quenching their drought in that vivifying stream; for what greater death can there be than not to know Thee, O Lord? They fall asleep in Thy soft and paternal bosom, and, full of the deceitful dreams by which they are tossed in their sleep, they are insensible of the powerful hand that supports them. If Thou wert a barren, impotent, and inanimate body, like a flower that fades away, a river that runs, a house that decays and falls to ruin, a picture that is but a collection of colours to strike the imagination, or a useless metal that glisters—they would perceive Thee, and fondly ascribe to Thee the power of giving them some pleasure, although in reality pleasure cannot proceed from inanimate beings, which are themselves void and incapable of it, but only from Thee alone, the true spring of all joy. If therefore Thou wert but a lumpish, frail, and inanimate being, a mass without any virtue or power, a shadow of a being, Thy vain fantastic nature would busy their vanity, and be a proper object to entertain their mean and brutish thoughts. But because Thou art too intimately within them, and they never at home, Thou art to them an unknown God; for while they rove and wander abroad, the intimate part of themselves is most remote from their sight. The order and beauty Thou scatterest over the face of Thy creatures are like a glaring light that hides Thee from and dazzles their sore eyes. Thus the very light that should light them strikes them blind; and the rays of the sun themselves hinder them to see it. In fine, because Thou art too elevated and too pure a truth to affect gross senses, men who are become like beasts cannot conceive Thee, though man has daily convincing instances of wisdom and virtue without the testimony of any of his senses; for those virtues have neither sound, colour, odour, taste, figure, nor any sensible quality. Why then, O my God, do men call Thy existence, wisdom, and power more in question than they do those other things most real and manifest, the truth of which they suppose as certain, in all the serious affairs of life, and which nevertheless, as well as Thou, escape our feeble senses? O misery! O dismal night that surrounds the children of Adam! O monstrous stupidity! O confusion of the whole man! Man has eyes only to see shadows, and truth appears a phantom to him. What is nothing, is all; and what is all, is nothing to him. What do I behold in all Nature? God. God everywhere, and still God alone. When I think, O Lord, that all being is in Thee, Thou exhaustest and swallowest up, O Abyss of Truth, all my thoughts. I know not what becomes of me. Whatever is not Thou, disappears; and scarce so much of myself remains wherewithal to find myself again. Who sees Thee not, never saw anything; and who is not sensible of Thee, never was sensible of anything. He is as if he were not. His whole life is but a dream. Arise, O Lord, arise. Let Thy enemies melt like wax and vanish like smoke before Thy face. How unhappy is the impious soul who, far from Thee, is without God, without hope, without eternal comfort! How happy he who searches, sighs, and thirsts after Thee! But fully happy he on whom are reflected the beams of Thy countenance, whose tears Thy hand has wiped off, and whose desires Thy love has already completed. When will that time be, O Lord? O Fair Day, without either cloud or end, of which Thyself shalt be the sun, and wherein Thou shalt run through my soul like a torrent of delight? Upon this pleasing hope my bones shiver, and cry out:—"Who is like Thee, O Lord? My heart melts and my flesh faints, O God of my soul, and my eternal wealth."

The Existence Of God

Francois Fenelon

www.ingramcontent.com/pod-product-compliance
Lightning Source LLC
Chambersburg PA
CBHW062035120526
44592CB00036B/2105